Robert Mayne Patterson

Elijah, the Favored Man

A Life and Its Lessons For Today

Robert Mayne Patterson

Elijah, the Favored Man
A Life and Its Lessons For Today

ISBN/EAN: 9783743383258

Manufactured in Europe, USA, Canada, Australia, Japa

Cover: Foto ©Lupo / pixelio.de

Manufactured and distributed by brebook publishing software (www.brebook.com)

Robert Mayne Patterson

Elijah, the Favored Man

THE FAVORED MAN.

A Life and its Lessons for To-day.

BY

ROBERT M. PATTERSON,

AUTHOR OF "PARADISE: THE PLACE AND STATE OF SAVED SOULS BETWEEN DEATH AND THE RESURRECTION;" "VISIONS OF HEAVEN FOR THE LIFE ON EARTH," ETC.

PHILADELPHIA:
PRESBYTERIAN BOARD OF PUBLICATION,
1334 CHESTNUT STREET.

WESTCOTT & THOMSON,
Stereotypers and Electrotypers, Philada.

INTRODUCTORY NOTE.

MUCH of the interest and power of the Bible is lost by an exclusive textual preaching and by fragmentary reading in verses or chapters.

We gain greatly by comprehensive views of one of its books or of one of its lives, and by reading therein the lessons for all time for which the record has been preserved. In the study of the inspired Word the microscope alone should not be used; the telescope brings to light beautiful and surprising discoveries.

Among the human lives of the Bible, that of Elijah stands on a peculiar plane. It is clothed with an interest in its simple story and in its suggestive instructions which is unapproachable by any other.

My object in this volume is to exhibit the biography itself in a clear and connected form; to deduce three of the most important series of permanent lessons for which, it seems to me, it was embalmed in the sacred Book; and to analyze the character of the man in order to ascertain wherein he should be a model for us all.

I hope the work will be found adapted not merely to Christians of advanced age, but to Sabbath-school members. The plot and incidents of a story pervade the scriptural narrative sufficiently to interest those whose taste has been unhappily developed in such a way as to receive entertainment and instruction only through the form of the novel; while its profounder revelations of God, of nature, of humanity, of redemption, cannot be exhausted by the lifelong study of the most advanced and thorough student.

It is not surprising that so much has been written and published in reference to this great and prominent character. But I am not aware that it has before been dealt with in the form which I have here adopted, or that it has been brought to bear upon modern life in the manner in which I employ it. Hence I venture to send the treatise forth with the prayer that the Spirit of God will bless it to the development of a type of piety which is greatly needed in our day and our land.

CONTENTS.

	PAGE
INTRODUCTORY NOTE	3

I.

THE LIFE	13-57
The Unique Position of Elijah	13
Preceding History of Israel	14
Ahab and Jezebel	16
Religion of Baal and Astarte	18
Scientific Skepticism of Our Day	21
Its Immoral Tendency	22
Secular Education	24
Persecution by Jezebel	26
Elijah's Early Life	29
His First Appearance	30
Description of him	30
His Message to Ahab	31
Withdrawal to Cherith	32
Fed by Ravens	33
Pigeons in St. Mark's, Venice	33
In Sarepta	35
Death and Resurrection of the Child	37

	PAGE
The Three Years' Drought...	38
The Struggle on Carmel...	41
The Flight...	45
Under the Juniper Tree...	46
At Mount Horeb...	47
God's Revelation of his Working...	48
Naboth...	49
Ahaziah and the Three Bands...	51
The Translation...	52
At the Transfiguration of Jesus...	54
The Perpetual Ministry...	55
"Alone"...	56

II.

GOD AND NATURE...	58–101
Elijah in the Presence of Ahab...	58
The Story in Brief...	59
Nature-Lessons:	
(1) God's Control over Nature...	67
The Doctrine of the Bible and of Science...	67
Uniformity of Nature...	68
Three Miraculous Bible Periods...	69
The Deliverance from Egypt...	69
Christ's Earthly Life...	69
Elijah and Elisha...	70
Every recorded Act of Elijah miraculous...	71
(2) Nature's Forces used for Moral Purposes...	76
The Physical and Moral Intermingled...	77
A False Judgment guarded against...	81
The Tower in Siloam...	81

CONTENTS.

	PAGE
The Galileans' Death	82
Job	83
Innocent Suffer here with Guilty	83
The Rule about Nations	84
Hence Responsibility of Private Citizens	85
Sins against Individuals grievous	88
Naboth's Case	88
Public Plunderers	89
(3) Natural Sufferings do not Reclaim	89
The Drought	90
The Carmel Judgment	90
Sentence for Sin against Naboth	90
Jezebel Hardened	91
Lord Byron	92
The Great Teaching of the Horeb Revelation	93
Of Elijah's Ministry contrasted with Christ's	95
The Conversation about the Samaritan Village	97
The Redeemer's Life and Mission	98
His Followers to Win by Kindness alone	99

III.

GOD'S WORK AND HIS AGENTS	102–137
Effect of Carmel Conflict:—	
On the People	102
On Ahab	102
On Jezebel	103
Her Threat	104
The Prophet Discouraged	105
The Various Explanations	107

	PAGE
A Natural Reaction	108
Exhibited in Others	110
Even in the Redeemer	111
God's Dealings with Elijah	112
Strengthened by Food and Sleep	112
By Communion with Nature	112
By Revelation of the True Church	113
By a Companion	114
By Refused Prayer for Death	114
(1) Breaks Permitted by God in his Work	116
Leaders Needed	116
The Slowness with which God works	121
(2) Apparent Failures	124
Elijah's Mission seemed a Failure	125
John the Baptist's	126
Christ's	127
But no Real Failure	128
The English Rebellion	129
(3) God's Tenderness toward the Depressed	134
Did not Reprove Elijah	134
Provides for his People	135

IV.

THE CHURCH AND IMMORTALITY	138–176
The Scriptural Kaleidoscope	138
New Testament References to Elijah	141
(1) The Church Indestructible	141
The Seven Thousand	142
England in Reformation Times	143

CONTENTS.

Europe under the Papacy	148
No Adherent of God is Alone	149
Obadiahs among Public Men	150
(2) The Catholicity of our Religion	151
The Widow of Sarepta	151
Jewish Narrowness	153
Salvation never Confined to Visible Church	154
Not in Ancient Times	154
Not Now	157
Intercourse with the Irreligious and Immoral	157
(3) Immortality	159
Old Testament Motives from Present Life	159
But Immortality Taught therein	162
Restoration of the Widow's Son	163
Translation of Elijah	165
Reappearance at Tabor	168
Death in the Midst of Work	171

V.

CHARACTER AND TRAINING OF THE MAN... 177-215

Malachi's Prophecy	177
John the Baptist	180
Influence of a Chivalrous Life	183
"Subject to Like Passions"	186
Varieties in Character	186
Elijah's Overmastering Devotion to God	188
(1) A Righteous Man	188
Therefore Powerful in Prayer	189
Especially Righteous toward God	191

	PAGE
Not a Weathercock	192
(2) His Piety Active	193
Passive Piety	193
Jealous for God, yet Gentle	195
Bunyan	197
(3) His Intrepid Courage	198
Yielding Men	199
Need of Faithful Courage	202
Its Possessors not Popular	203
The Basis of Elijah's Character:	
1. Great Physical Strength	204
Influence of Body on Mind	204
Voltaire	205
Samuel Johnson	206
Nerves	208
Abstinence from Vice	208
From Intoxicating Liquors	209
2. Private Meditation and Prayer	209
Rest a Necessity	211
Study of God's Word	213
"Greater than Elijah"	215

ELIJAH, THE FAVORED MAN.

I.

THE LIFE.

THE prophet Elijah has been called "the grandest and the most romantic character that Israel ever produced." He bursts upon the sacred page with the suddenness of a meteor; he shines high up as a star of the first magnitude in the kingdom of heaven for ever. Because of his character and his work he was exalted by God to an eminence to which no other man has been advanced. He is one of the two human beings who never died, but were translated to the glory of heaven without suffering the infliction of sin's sharpest sting—Enoch being the other. He was also one of the two who came down from heaven on the night of Christ's transfiguration on earth, and amid the preternatural splendor of the mount communed with the Redeemer about his approaching exodus—Moses being the other. Thus favored with Enoch in the one way, and with Moses in the other, he was distinguished as each of them was not.

Our attention is therefore challenged to him as the most extraordinary of the sons of men. The Elijah of the Old Testament, the Elias of the New (the first is the Hebrew form of his name, the second the Greek), he is, in his person, his life, his mission, worthy of careful study, that we may learn what in him was exceptional and what may be imitated.

When this magnificent man made his appearance upon the stage of the sacred history the kingdom of Israel had existed for sixty-five years. The heinous sin of Jeroboam, the first king of that schismatic government, had been working out its legitimate results.* After a reign of twenty-two years Jeroboam had been succeeded by his son Ahijah; but in fulfillment of God's threatened judgment on account of the crime of his father, Ahijah and all his relatives were in two years destroyed by a conspirator, Baasha. The successful regicide sat upon the throne for twenty-four years, and was followed by Elah his son, who in two years was assassinated, in a drunken fit, by one of his officers, Zimri, who also destroyed all the other descendants of Baasha because of his sins. Zimri, in return, after a phosphorescent glow of seven days, was overcome by Omri, who

* It ought to be noted, as having a significancy for all time, that under Jeroboam " the defection of Israel did not consist in rejecting Jehovah as a false god, or in renouncing the Law of Moses as a false religion, but in joining foreign worship and idolatrous ceremonies to the ritual of the true God."—*Warburton's Divine Legation*, b. v., sec. 3.

was called to the throne by the army. The people, however, divided in the choice. Half of them followed another man, Tibni; but after a six years' civil war Omri and his faction conquered, and for six years he reigned as undisputed king. Thus a succession of internal convulsions racked the state and blasted its prospects.

Omri plunged the nation very decidedly down the inclined plane of religious declension. Jeroboam, the first king, had established an unscriptural worship, had himself participated in it, and had thus thrown the influence of his authority and example in favor of his gross departure from the religion which God had prescribed. But Omri seems to have gone further, and by law to have compelled the people to adopt this false worship.

Thus swayed by royal example and coerced by illegally-legal enactments, the nation was weakened and prepared for the terrific plunge which it took under

Ahab, the son of Omri, who reigned for twenty-two years. Down to his time Jehovah had been nominally recognized, though worshiped in a forbidden manner; under him Jehovah was repudiated utterly, and the vilest of heathen and vicious religions was enthroned and established in the Holy Land.

The sweeping record about Ahab is: "Ahab the son of Omri did evil in the sight of the Lord above all that were before him. And it came to pass, as if it had been a light thing for him to walk in the sins of Jeroboam the son of Nebat, that he took to wife Jezebel the daughter of Ethbaal king of the Zidonians, and went and served Baal, and worshiped him. And he reared up an altar for Baal in the house of Baal, which he had built in Samaria. And Ahab made a grove; and Ahab did more to provoke the Lord God of Israel to anger than all the kings of Israel that were before him." 1 Kings xvi. 30–33.

Thus a woman who had been born in a licentious heathen house was elevated to the highest seat in Israel, and all the energy of her soul was used "to eradicate the worship of Jehovah and establish the rites of her own national deities, Baal and Astarte."

Baal, the sun; Astarte, the moon—the male and the female, the generative and the receptive powers of nature—these were the deities which in the Phœnician Tyre and Sidon had been exalted to the throne of religious worship.

The religion was one which was quite widespread in the East, and was the more prevalent because "its real strength lay in the appeal it made to man's worst passions. Its root-idea seems to have been a worship of natural power and of material force; while, practically, its service was a consecration of vice and filth under the guise of reverence for the teeming life and glory of the universe."

"No form of idolatry could have been more fearfully the opposite of all that God had desired for his people. A worship of Nature, of mere strength and power—such is the meaning of Baal, rather than faith in a righteous will governing nature for moral purposes—brought with it, as it ever must, the most degrading consequences. The uncleanness which formed so great a part of the authorized worship, and which stood in such woeful contrast to the rigorous washing from all defilement enjoined by the Mosaic law, is but a symbol of the tendency of all Nature-worship in whatever form it may gain ascendency. The service of Baalim, gross as it was, yet may find a true counterpart in modern times. Let men permit their minds to be so overwhelmed by the thought of the vast forces which acquaintance with physical laws informs us of as to see nothing in Nature but the regular fulfillment of a great mechanism, so fixed and inexorable that the workings of the divine will, ruling for moral purposes, must cease to be believed in; let the same reasoning which is applied to blind material forces be introduced into the region of morals, and the value of personal will be denied,—then fatalism must ensue, and all that we do or feel be regarded as but a necessary result over which we have no control: we shall worship force, not God, a system, not a righteous Father; responsibility will become illogical, for evil must then be viewed as forming a part of a great plan; and the grand practical result of such one-sided science will be in the end none other than that of the basest of old creature-worships, the being given up to vile affections. We are entering on this inclined plane when, denying the sphere of miracle as the coming in of a divine will for righteous ends, we subject the moral to the material; and the chain of logic which leads thence to irresponsibility consists of but few links.

Baal, the lord of force, ever sits enthroned beside Astarte the licentious."*

This is the charge which we make against the materialism of the skeptical yet credulous scientists of the day—against the Nature-worship of which men like Tyndall and Huxley are the high priests. It is the successor, though higher in form and as yet restrained from its practical moral debasement, of Baal the sun-god, the god of force. Indeed, the first catchword of this modern system is *Force*, FORCE—the Force which in varying forms runs through nature, constitutes nature, causes all the transformations of existence. It is a force, too, which has its mighty seat in the sun, and which in a stern, inexorable, undeviating progress has been evolving itself through all the past and shall be through all the future. Blind, blind nature! potential forces marching on with remorseless tread! This system does not make all its

* The Rev. Donald McLeod in *Sunday Magazine*, i., 860.

advocates impure and immoral. It has its higher intellectual side, which leads captive a few who study nature alone. But so had the old horrid system of Jezebel "an esoteric meaning for the cultured and the initiated," which gave it a "fascinating power" over them. It had its "mystic meanings, through which the more thoughtful minds sought to sublimate the evil into an occult philosophy." Through the mass of its adherents, however, and especially down through the rude, the uncultured, and the unrestrained, it spread the very leprosy of impurity. Similar would be the result of the widespread prevalence of its scientific successor of modern times.*

---

* It is humiliating to human nature that the irreligious science of the day, which tramples on the divine Jesus, has not advanced beyond the teachings of the Roman Lucretius, who died about half a century before Jesus was born. Thus, Mallock, in his *Lucretius* (p. 161), says: "If we consider the general result of his teaching, his first principles and his last conclusions—if we consider these as he taught them, and not the ways by which he arrived at and supported them—we shall see that, as far as these go, his message to the world and that of modern science is prac-

Two of the careful scientific men of the day open a treatise which they have lately published with the confession of this truth. Individual immortality is one of the fundamental doctrines of a true spiritual religion. It is a doctrine, however, which the scientific heresy denies. And these writers candidly say: "The great mass of mankind have always believed, in some fashion, in the immortality of the soul; but it is certain that we may find disbelievers in this doc-

tically identical. Human life, in both systems, is the same momentary phenomenon in the great and everchanging evolution of things. It is the result of a power that knew not what it did in creating it. A little while it is, and again a little while and it is not. It is but a bubble on the surface of the great flux of matter. It is an isolated thing, connected with no interests beyond itself. It is to be judged of and ordered with reference to itself solely. It is to be valued solely on account of its present resources, and all these resources are to be expressed in terms of conscious and of realized happiness. Lucretius says this as distinctly, and thought he could prove it as surely, as Professor Huxley or Auguste Comte. In relation to human life, then—in relation, that is, to the thing that alone gives anything any interest for us—the materialism of Lucretius and the materialism of our own day are in exactly the same position."

trine who retain the nobler attributes of humanity. It may, however, be questioned if it be possible even to imagine the great bulk of our race to have lost their belief in the soul's immortality and yet to have retained the virtues of civilized and well-ordered communities." *

Nothing could be more disastrous in its influence, moral and political, on the mass of the people, than the adoption and prevalence of the strictly secular principle of education in our school and collegiate system. Let revealed truths be utterly ignored; let the teachings of science be circulated in forms which contain nature and its operations without any reference to the divine power which is in, through and above nature; let the instruction all be about the forces of matter as if they were fatalized developments — and the masses of the people would soon be in a position that would parallel the condition of the

* *The Unseen Universe*, p. 1.

subjects of the old Baal- and Astarte-worship. The foundation of all moral law would be swept away, and the multitude would grow more vile than the French Communists ever were. One of the great lessons taught by Grecian history is that mere intellectual knowledge does not purify the heart and moralize the life. It "showed to all future time the weakness of man's highest powers if unassisted from above." *

Ahab and Jezebel introduced the low and vicious system of Nature-religion into the kingdom of Israel. It became the court religion. Splendid temples were erected as the seats of its worship. Images of its goddess, Ashtoreth, abounded. Four hundred and fifty of its priests were scattered through the land to seduce the people to it. Four hundred more were supported at the table of the queen. The foul leprosy, whitening the walls of the royal palace in

* Conybeare and Howson, i. 11.

Samaria, extended itself over all the land and down to all ranks. Compulsion was also resorted to for the purpose of extending it. The first religious persecution that we read of in the history of the world was in its interest.

Christian sects have time and again disgraced themselves by endeavoring to compel others to embrace their tenets and by dealing cruelly with those who would not do so. But in that they departed from the essential spirit of the gospel. They learned it, moreover, from heathenism. The law of Moses was not persecuting in its nature. From the first, heathen could dwell in the promised land and under the protection of the inspired code without being compelled to become Jews in religion. The laws of Christ do not persecute. As the papacy was developed it exhibited the taint of Roman heathenism, which had, at an earlier day, persecuted Christians. Protestants who have persecuted were overcome by the leaven of the heathenism and the papacy which remained in them.*

Under Ahab and Jezebel there was a most bitter persecution of the worshipers of Jehovah. Then commenced what Nehemiah in his prayer four hundred and fifty years later referred to: "Nevertheless, they were disobedient and rebelled against thee, and cast thy law behind their backs, and slew thy prophets, which testified against them to turn them to thee, and they wrought great provocations." Jezebel "cut off the prophets of the Lord." She tried to make a clean sweep of them,

* Dean Stanley, in his *History of the Eastern Church* (p. 339, Am. ed.), calls attention to the fact that the first persecution of Christian by Christian "arose not from the orthodox against the orthodox, but from the heretics against the orthodox." The treatment to which the great Athanasius was subjected, he says, furnishes "the first signal instance of the strange sight of Christians persecuting Christians." He adds (p. 349), "that it was a maxim of Athanasius that 'the duty of orthodoxy is not to compel, but to persuade, belief.'" Even Lecky confesses (*History of Rationalism in Europe*, ii. 22), that "in this respect the orthodox seem to have been for a time honorably distinguished even from the Arians."

and it was only by a shrewd and dangerous device of Obadiah, the governor of the king's household, who remained faithful at the court, that any of them were preserved. He rescued a hundred of them, and hid them in two caves, and by stealth fed them with bread and water. So destructive was the work of the persecutors, so subservient seemed the people, and so universally did they appear to adopt the false religion, that Elijah thought he was the only person who remained true to the divine cause. And when God disabused his mind of that impression, all that the Omniscient One could say was that there were seven thousand people in all the land who had not bowed to Baal. Of the more than four million inhabitants who composed the nation, all except seven thousand had either yielded to the blandishments of error, and with the heart received it, or by fear of suffering and death had professed to yield to it.

Thus the nation had gone down into a pit of horrid blackness. The true religion had been overthrown. A licentious system had been enthroned in its place. The cancer of a vile and filthy immorality disfigured and was eating out the life of the land.

Elijah the Tishbite was living in the country east of the Jordan, and farthest from the influence of the apostate court. In solitude he was brooding over the degradation of his people. His stern theocratic soul waxed indignant and rose in holy rebellion against the despotism of vice. The energy of his nature first found utterance in the prayer that Jehovah would interpose and maintain his own cause. As against that religion of force which was exalting itself, he prayed that a drought and a famine might sweep down upon the land to bring the people to their senses. The prayer was God's own inspiration. The prophet believed that it would be answered.

Suddenly, after Ahab had been eight or ten years on the throne, the trans-Jordanic messenger from God broke into the presence of the sinful king. The apparition must have been a repulsive one to the dainty eye of the monarch who had erected and lived in an ivory palace and who dressed in purple and fared sumptuously.

Bring together and behold the descriptions which are given in different places of the appearance of Elijah, so as to get a definite view of his person and manner of life:

"Long, shaggy hair floating over his back, and a large rough mantle of sheepskin fastened around his loins by a girdle of hide was his only covering." His figure was awful and wild; his countenance and his voice were stern and unbroken; his garb was "scanty."

Not attractive in appearance, surely! Not such a man as society would with pleasure receive into its circle! Not at all pleasant to the dainty and silken Ahab. But the style of man that God has used in times of deep declension and odious vice to startle and shock communities. John the Baptist, Luther, Knox, somewhat in the same mould, have been sent into the world from time to time.

The message which the prophet announced to the king was more alarming than his appearance. For three years and six months neither rain nor dew should bless the land. As the court and the people had accepted the idol-worship of the sun, the furnace of all earth's forces, God would show that he controlled that sun, and could use it as a burning agent to punish those who had deified it. For three and a half years the face of the scorching luminary should never be hidden from view by day, nor, in her season, should the moon by night be covered by any mantle. No clouds should float through the air or drop their golden globules of wealth and comfort. Neither rain nor snow should descend upon the land to cool and fructify it. No dew-pearls should lightly rest upon the turf. The rivers and streamlets should dry up. The fruits of the earth should fail. The grass should be scorched, burned, destroyed. Men and cattle should lose their subsistence. Very terrible indeed in the hand of the Creator would be the sun and its stored-up forces to rebuke those who had enthroned it as a god.

The man who carried such a message to royal ears could not be safe within the reach of the strong-minded and blood-thirsty heatheness who, with an iron rod, ruled her weak-minded husband, and his perverted subjects as well. Therefore, God commanded Elijah to hide himself while the judgment was slowly and inexorably working itself out upon the land.

First, he retired to the neighborhood of a brook running into the Jordan, and there every morning and evening fed upon bread and flesh which ravens, against the instinct of their nature, but under the controlling influence of their Maker, brought to him.

In the Place of St. Mark, Venice, we once saw flocks of pigeons, which, by nature timid and ready to fly away at the sound of a human step near them, had been so trained by men that, at the stroke of the bell, at two o'clock in the afternoon of every day, they flew from all quarters to a particular window in a corner of the place to be fed on corn as it was rained out upon them. We saw them not merely flutter around the window to receive their supply from well-known hands, but drop down fearlessly among the spectators who from various parts of the world had gathered together to witness the scene. A dozen at a time hopped upon our knees, and crept up upon our shoulders, and picked the corn from our hands. Seeing, in that, one instance of *man's* power over birds of the air, we have no trouble in believing that God could so employ the ravens—whose habits were carnivorous, living on flesh and seeking for it everywhere, and which the Mosaic law did not permit to be eaten by its subjects—as to make them daily carry necessary food to one of his famishing servants.

It is one of the shameful and sinful comicalities of a skeptical interpretation of God's book that a writer has advanced the idea that Elijah merely plundered the ravens' nests of hares and other game, and thus was fed by them. The inspired history "knows nothing of bird-catching and nest-robbing, but acknowledges the Lord and Creator of the creatures, who *commanded the ravens* to provide his servant with bread and flesh."

But it came to pass after a while that for want of rain the brook from which Elijah drank dried up. It was necessary for him to go elsewhere.

Away, then, from the lonely retirement of a recluse amid "the bare, desolate hills of the wilderness of Judea, in whose fastnesses David had been able to bid defiance to Saul"—away to a city, but, strange to say, a city in the heathen country of Sidon, from which the infamous queen had come! As he approached its gate, wayworn, thirsty and faint, he met a widow whose heart God inclined to deal generously with him. She gave him a cup of the cold water that had not yet failed in that region, and though, in her despair, having only a handful of meal in a jar and a little oil in a cruse, she was hunting sticks to make a fire wherewith she might cook what she supposed would be the last meal for herself and her only son, still, on the strength of the prophet's assurance that her little supply should not fail, but should keep on reproducing itself until the return of the blessing of rain, she made him first a little cake. His promise was fulfilled. The woman entertained the prophet, and the God of the prophet kept her supply unexhausted.*

* " Is thy cruse of comfort failing? Rise and share it with another,
    And through all the years of famine it shall serve thee and thy brother.
    Love divine will fill thy storehouse or thy handful still renew;
    Scanty fare for one will often make a royal feast for two.

" For the heart grows rich in giving; all its wealth is living grain :
    Seeds which mildew in the garner, scattered, fill with gold the plain.
    Is thy burden hard and heavy? Do thy steps drag wearily?
    Help to bear thy brother's burden; God will bear both it and thee.

" Numb and weary on the mountains, wouldst thou sleep amidst the snow?
    Chafe that frozen form beside thee, and together both shall glow.
    Art thou stricken in life's battle? Many wounded round thee moan ;
    Lavish on their wounds thy balsam, and that balm shall heal thine own.

" Is the heart a well left empty? None but God its void can fill;
    Nothing but a ceaseless fountain can its ceaseless longings still.

A year had passed when a sad event happened in the hospitable home. The poor widow's boy fell sick and died. The affliction quickened the mother's memory of her sinful life. She looked upon the blow as a judgment on account of transgression, and upbraided the prophet for having been the instrument in bringing the infliction upon her. But, taking the cold body in his bony arms to his own room, as he had by prayer closed the windows of heaven in wrath upon his sinful land, so he by the same power brought life back to the boy and restored him to the arms of the mourning parent.

It is interesting to note, though we place not the statement on a level with the clear facts which are imbedded in the inspired pages, and are not called upon to receive it implicitly, that tradition identified this

> Is the heart a living power? Self-entwined, its strength sinks low;
> It can only live in loving, and by serving love will grow."—
> *The Women of the Gospel, and Other Poems*, p. 181.

child of the widow of Zarephath (Sarepta), the boy who attended Elijah to the wilderness after the conflict on Carmel, the youth who anointed Jehu by the direction of Elisha, and the prophet Jonah, as one and the same. "In this boy (so later ages delighted to believe) was recovered the first prophet of the Gentile world, Jonah, the son of Amittai; repaying, in his mission of mercy and pity to the Assyrian Nineveh, the mercy and pity which his mother had shown to the Israelite wanderer."*

For three years Elijah remained concealed in his foreign shelter. The drought continued. "Week after week, month after month, the blazing sun rose and sunk without a cloud. Season gave place to season, yet no change until that most frightful of Eastern scourges, want of water, fell with all its dire consequences. Each day the heavens were as brass, the horizon dim with the haze of heat, the sun an eye of

* Stanley's *History of the Jewish Church*, ii. 331.

fire, the earth baked and cracked and hard as iron. Night after night, over a dry and dewless earth, rose that moon, sacred sign of Ashtoreth, bringing no relief to those who hymned her cold beauty. Day after day, that sun, symbol of Baal, burned down like a vengeance on his worshippers."*

Horrid famine followed, stalking with its gaunt form through country and town, and at last entering even the richly-provided royal city. The regal supplies gave out. The pampered horses and mules of the king's stables were dying. Ahab and Obadiah divided the land between them, in order to pick from the water-line of any fountains or brooks that might not yet have been entirely dried up grass enough to save the horses that were still alive.

No humbling effect, however, seems to have been produced by the long-continued judgment on the court or people. Another

* *Sunday Magazine*, i. 863.

move must be made in the campaign that was being waged.

While the prophet kept himself hidden in retirement Ahab had been making persistent and varied efforts to find him. Elijah had declared that rain should only come according to his word. Doubtless the king sought " to get him into his power, with the view of either inflicting vengeance upon him or of endeavoring to compel him to procure the desired blessing." Therefore, he made the most earnest inquisition in all the kingdoms round for the abiding-place of the man whom he considered to be the troubler of Israel.

But now the time had arrived for the prophet, under God's direction, to show himself voluntarily to the suffering but incensed monarch, and to fight a battle which should condense into one day, and in a more fiery manner, the great truths which the gradual judgment of three and a half years should have burned into the national mind

From the quiet home in Zarephath the story therefore transports us to Mount Carmel, one of Nature's grand scenes, overlooking the blue and glittering Mediterranean Sea to the west, and the valley of Jezreel, the fairest portion of the Holy Land, and one of the great battle-fields of the world, to the east. The prophet had directed the king, when he encountered him on his return from Zarephath, to summon the priests of Baal and of the grove to meet him there, that between them a mighty spiritual duel might be fought which should show to the Israelites who ought to be recognized as their Lord. The four hundred and fifty prophets of Baal responded to the summons. The four hundred of the groves who lived at Jezebel's table, perhaps influenced by her or suspecting the object and confident of their failure, did not put in an appearance.

Then came one of the stirring events in the history of the world. The king, the false prophets and the representatives of the people were gathered together before the shaggy and stern minister of God. He taunted the multitude with their halting gait between the worship of the true deity, whom they had never formally renounced, and that of Baal, to whom they had been seduced in practice. Then he challenged the priests of Baal to a contest of fire—he on one side, the four hundred and fifty on the other! Let him and them each take a bullock and in turn call upon the God whom they honored, and let the power who should send down fire from heaven to consume the sacrifice be recognized as the true God and with the whole heart be obeyed!

Forced into the trial by the approval of the people, the four hundred and fifty Baalites prepared their bullock for the sacrifice. In the early morning, as their sun-god rose above the horizon, they called upon him to hear them. As he burned upon them from the zenith they reiterated their cry. As he slowly moved downward toward the western horizon with no answering voice or sign, they danced around the altar and cut themselves with knives and lancets, in the agony of their prayer, until their blood gushed out, while Elijah mocked them with a cutting irony about the possible habits of their god: "Cry aloud: for he is a god; either he meditateth, or he is pursuing, or he is in a journey, or peradventure he sleepeth and must be awaked." But the burning red ball sank out of sight beyond the Mediterranean, leaving the bullock unconsumed, untouched.

Elijah erected his altar, and having drenched it and the bullock and the wood and the ditch around it with water, so as to preclude all idea of a collusive proceeding, he called upon Jehovah, the covenant God of Israel, to show that he was indeed God, and that the petitioner his prophet was acting according to his word. And scarcely ascended the words of the prayer from his lips ere the fire of the Lord descended and consumed the burnt sacrifice and the wood and the stones and the dust, and licked up the water that was in the trench.

The victory was complete. The people shouted the verdict. Under the command of the inspired man as the executioner of God's will, they slew the false and treasonable prophets.

Then Elijah announced to the paralyzed king that the unparalleled drought was at an end. And as the chariot of the monarch hastened toward Jezreel, with the prophet running at its side, the heavens became black with clouds and there was a great rain.

The enthusiasm of the people for the Jehovah of their fathers had been kindled anew by the fire from heaven. Perhaps the king also had been swept along on the wave of feeling. But the imperious queen remained unsubdued and defiant. Madly thirsting for the blood of the man of God, or, it may be, desiring to terrify him into a flight from the court and the city, where he would certainly possess potential influence after such a triumph, she sent him word that before to-morrow's sun went down his head should bite the dust. The prophet of fire and of undoubted courage was for once, and for the only time, cowed, and that by a woman's threat. "And he feared, and arose, and went for his life." Perhaps it is not to be wondered at. He was a man of like passions with ourselves. His human nature had passed through an excitement which was necessarily followed by a reaction. The exhausted body weakened the mind. He feared and he fled.

Doubtless, his flight set back the work of reformation. The people were left without a leader, and sank down again into their idolatry.

"It was the crisis of his life." Only one out of that vast multitude who the day before shouted after the fire-miracle, "The Lord, he is God! the Lord, he is God!" (we forget not how at a later day a similar multitude, who shouted Hosanna as Jesus entered Jerusalem, in a few hours cried, "Crucify him! crucify him!")—only one "remained faithful to him, the Zidonian boy of Zarephath, as Jewish tradition believed"—the boy whom he had brought back from death, and who afterward became the prophet Jonah.

Without stopping to think of the effects of his absence at such a critical time, Elijah hastened from Jezreel. Down through Israel and Judah he sped. The first night of his flight he rested under a broom tree, and in his depression of spirits asked the Lord to cut short his life. But, first, God gave his belóved, though temporarily despondent, servant a refreshing sleep, and, afterward, by an angel, supplied him with bread and water, by which his strength was recuperated. Then onward again he went to the south-west, unto Mount Horeb, renowned in the history of Israel for its associations with Moses, the first revealer of the will of the Most High.

There the Lord made to the prophet a remarkable typical representation of the real mode and force by which he works in the advancement of his cause. The exile had been disappointed. He had hoped that the fire which came down upon Carmel would burn away the false religion from the hearts of the nation, perhaps even melt the hard heart of the idolatrous queen. She had, however, remained rampant in her hatred of the true worship. And he had fled. He was jealous for Jehovah, but he stood alone and his life was sought. His ministry had been a failure. Force had been vain.

One cannot stand against a multitude. "None follow him, and he is left alone, flying for his life from the sword which has slain his brethren." But as he stood upon the mount a great and strong wind rent the mountains and broke in pieces the rocks before the Lord. An earthquake upheaved the mountain from its base. The lightning burst forth and wrapped the wild scene in a blaze. Neither in the wind, the earthquake nor the fire, however, was the Lord. But, following them, a still small voice! and that was the effective power of the Most High. Not by natural judgments, even the most terrifying and destructive, does he subdue and convert men, but by his gentle, gracious influence.

Then he indicated to the prophet that his work would not fail in the end, though the successful result might not appear to him. And he commissioned him to seek and anoint as his successor Elisha, who in turn should anoint a new king of Israel and a new king of Syria, who would after a while be the instruments of God in dealing with the obdurate house of Ahab. Nor was the cause of God as weak as the desponder thought. There were seven thousand who stood upright among the faithless.

After finding Elisha in obedience to this command, Elijah vanished for about six years from the public history of Israel; while Ahab, with varying fortunes, was prosecuting war against the king of Syria.

But once more, and for the last time, the prophet and the king were brought face to face. The monarch had shown that he was craven-hearted and vacillating in military matters as he had been weak and false in religion. As a man he further showed himself to be grasping. Hard by his palace in Jezreel was a vineyard belonging to a private Israelite. The covetous eye of royalty fell upon it, but its owner would not agree either to a sale or an exchange. The king moped and became melancholy because he could not secure it. The queen came to his help. She devised a high-handed and iniquitous conspiracy by which, on a charge of blasphemy, the owner of the vineyard was put to death with his family. The property was forfeited to the Crown. Ahab with a glad heart took possession. But while he was surveying it with the pride of recent acquisition in his eye, Elijah confronted him, by the order of God, and announced the disgraceful death of himself, his wife and all his family: the dogs of the city and the fowl of the air would feed upon their flesh. On the spot where Naboth had been illegally stoned to death should the dogs lick up the blood of Ahab.

A temporary spasm of remorse agitated the frame of the wretched man. But he went on to his fate. In two years more he was killed in battle.

Ahaziah his son succeeded him, and followed in the footsteps of his father and mother in the worship of Baal and its attendant vices. In the second year of his reign, meeting with an accident, he sent to inquire of an idol god whether he should recover from the effects of it. Again Elijah crosses the path of the public history. Intercepting the messengers, he directed them to return to the king with the declaration that because he had thus contemptuously treated Jehovah he should never rise from his bed, but should surely die. The sick man, obdurate and indignant, sent a band of fifty men to secure the person of the prophet. Something in their mien or bearing led Elijah to call down fire from heaven for their destruction. A second band, approaching in the same spirit, met with the same reception. With a third band, who advanced in a different manner, he returned to the king and repeated his sentence; and "so he died, according to the word of the Lord which Elijah had spoken."

About thirteen years—so brief was his public ministry—had passed since Elijah first stood in the presence of Ahab. His immediate work was done. The hour for his crowning had arrived. After first making a circuit of the schools of the prophets, accompanied by Elisha, he crossed the Jordan to his native district. He separated the waters with a stroke of his mantle, which he was in the habit of wrapping together as a staff, and walked over on dry ground. Then, as the master and his divinely-appointed successor moved on in earnest conversation, "nearly at the same spot where Moses had vanished from the eyes of his countrymen" a chariot of fire and horses of fire parted them asunder, and the prophet of fire went up by a whirlwind into heaven, and Elisha saw him no more.

Of course it was from this that the Scotch poet derived the splendid imagery in which he described the death of the old Covenanters upon one of their battle-fields:

> "When the righteous had fallen, and the combat was ended,
> A chariot of fire through the dark cloud descended;
> Its drivers were angels on horses of whiteness,
> And its burning wheels turned on axles of brightness.
>
> "A seraph unfolded its doors bright and shining,
> All dazzling like gold of the seventh refining;
> And the souls that came forth out of great tribulation
> Have mounted the chariot and steeds of salvation."

Up above the clouds, above the stars that appear to us, above the whole expanse of the visible universe, into the place of exceeding brightness and glory where God has his throne, and where the home of the angels is, Elijah passed, soul and body unseparated—into the innermost circle of the glorified; into blissful communion with Abraham, Isaac, Jacob, Moses and all the heroes of the race who had been faithful to their God; into ecstatic converse with the Son of God himself, who had been using him as one of the mighty instruments of his redemptive work.

The young men in the school of the prophets sent out fifty men, who searched the mountains and the valleys for three days to see if they could find his body. But in vain: that body, glorified, was enjoying the rapture of heaven with Enoch, who in the dawn of human history had also been translated without seeing death. Among all who thus far have left the earth Enoch and Elijah diverse from the rest appear:

> "Their form
> Is that of men, and yet not mortal men;
> Their likeness spiritual, yet not spirits alone,
> So pure the texture of that robe they wear,
> The light translucent through transfigured flesh,
> As onyx stone or ruby flashing fire."

Over nine hundred years passed in the enjoyment of that blissful rest, and again the prophet appeared upon the earth. With Moses he winged his way down to meet the Redeemer in the flesh, and on the Mount of Transfiguration conversed with him about that exodus which was to turn the death of all the redeemed into a translation from earth to heaven.

Though Elijah then disappeared again as suddenly as he had appeared, his ministry ceased not. John the Baptist came in the spirit and power of Elias. Wherever men are deeply sunken in sin, and need to have an overmastering repentance preached, the same spirit and power are at work. If the expectation of the bodily return of the prophet before the second advent of the Lord be too literal an interpretation of the revealed word, the spirit of the same ministry shall introduce the supreme event of human history.

Here is a biography which stands alone in the literature of the Church and of the world. The time and the place of the man's birth unknown; an eventful, far-reaching ministry of thirteen years, during which his word "burned like a lamp;" no end to the life, but a whirlwind ascent to the city of our God, the new Jerusalem of glory!

And what is the one great lesson whose glow is over it all? It is this:

Be devoted to the true God and to his service, whoever else refuses to stand with you. Be faithful to him, and he will carry you through the struggles of the world; and, though your frame may pass under the form of death, your soul will be translated to the place of exceeding glory, and at last, with reclaimed body, will be ravished by the complete joy of redemption.

Alone! alone! Was Elijah really alone? No; not then, not now. He belonged, and belongs, to a glorious company. "Oh, Elias!" cries out the writer of one of the apocryphal books, "how wast thou honored in thy wondrous deeds! And who may glory like unto thee? . . . Blessed are they that saw thee and slept in love; for we shall surely live." Be of their number. Remain not among the Baal-worshipers. Live not in the world of those who refuse to look above nature. Mingle not with those who indulge in the world's vices. Come out from among them, and be ye separate. Follow the Lord for whom Elijah was jealous. In that service be intensely zealous to the end, and you will at last wear a crown of life with Enoch and Moses and Elijah, and, more than all, with the divine Jesus himself! Tabernacle with them now, and with them you will abide for evermore.

II.
GOD AND NATURE.

ABRUPT and dramatic was the manner in which Elijah appeared upon the sacred page. Without a preparatory note of warning, he stood in the presence of the apostate king and uttered a sentence which embodied the essence of his mission: "As the Lord God of Israel liveth, before whom I stand, there shall not be dew nor rain these years, but according to my word." 1 Kings xvii. 1. He was the servant of the Lord God of Israel; and by the omnipotent One he had been clothed with an influence over Nature which was to be used for the infliction of judgment upon the nation and upon its rulers for their aggravated sins.

In the preceding chapter I endeavored, in a pictorial style, with the aid of side-lights, and with references here and there to our own condition, to tell the wonderful story of this prophet of fire. I gathered, from the different parts of the word of God in which it is contained, the biography of the man and his relation to the apostate kingdom of Israel—a biography which no intelligent person can read or hear without having the heart set on fire.

It may deepen the impression which the longer narrative has made, and will the more vividly prepare for the great permanent lessons for which the biography was embalmed in the inspired Book and has been preserved for all ages, if I condense in a still more compact form the great facts of the life.

Elijah appeared nearly two thousand eight hundred years ago, nine hundred years before our divine Saviour was born on the earth, and about sixty-five years after the Hebrew commonwealth, through the supreme folly of Solomon's son, and as a judgment for the sins into which the magnificent monarch had fallen and led the nation, had been divided.

The separatist kingdom of Israel had been plunged into the gulf of one of the vilest of religions. An idolatress of the worst and most imperious cast was its queen. Her infamous religion had been forced upon the nation, and persecution had been inaugurated to compel the people to receive it.

On account of that, and in answer to his inspired prayer, Elijah was sent by God to declare to the king that a drought should for three and a half years curse the land.

During that infliction the prophet was specially cared for by God; first, near a brook running into the Jordan in the territory of the kingdom of Judah, where, day by day, he was miraculously fed by ravens; then in a town of the heathen Sidon, in the home of a widow whose scanty supply of food was kept from failing, and whose boy he called back from the region of death.

At the end of that period he again appeared to Ahab the king and had a remarkable contest with four hundred and fifty priests of the idolatrous religion. *They* failed to bring fire from the sun to burn the sacrifice that had been placed on their altar; in response to *his* prayer Jehovah's lightning struck and consumed not only his sacrifice, but the altar itself, and evoked from the multitude the thundering shout, "Jehovah, he is God! Jehovah, he is God!"

Having executed judicial vengeance upon the false prophets, Elijah announced to the king that the drought was at an end; and then the monarch in his chariot and the prophet on foot ran from Carmel to Jezreel, the royal summer city, under the pelting of a great rain, every drop of which was better than gold to the scorched and cracked soil.

The bad queen, however, was furious at

the truthful but rough man of God. She threatened him with death. He fled, weakly and unhappily, to the Arabian desert and to the mount of Moses. For once in his life fearful and discouraged, he abandoned his post and lost his vantage-ground.

But God pitied the human weakness which was the physical and mental reaction of the hard ordeal through which his servant had passed. Beneath a juniper tree on the way he sent his angel to refresh the exhausted man with sleep and to strengthen him with food; and afterward, on the mount, made a revelation which showed him that the divine cause was not as weak in the nation as he thought, and that his work should not fail in the end, though success was not to come in the way and at the time that he had expected.

Then, by divine direction, Elijah anointed Elisha as his successor to carry on his work after his departure.

Six years passed with the prophet in retirement. The king and the queen doubtless thought they were free from him. The fruits of the Carmel victory remained ungathered. So debased had the leaders of the people become that the foreign heatheness was able to use them as instruments in trumping up a false charge of blasphemy against a private citizen, in order to destroy him and his family, and to give to the king the vineyard on which he had cast covetous eyes, but which the owner had refused either to sell or exchange. This atrocious act of spoliation and murder brought the prophet from his obscurity into the presence of Ahab, and led him to denounce sweeping and disgraceful deaths against the royal pair and all their descendants.

In two years the judgment fell upon Ahab. Following him, his son Ahaziah was met by Elijah and told that he also should die because he had treated Jehovah with despite.

Shortly after that, and about thirteen years from the day when he had first stepped upon the page of the sacred history, Elijah was translated to the glory of heaven. He did not die. On a whirlwind he was borne in triumph to the beautiful land. For nine hundred years he enjoyed the bliss of immediate communion with the redeemed who had gone up, and through the ages were going up, from the struggles of earth to the bright mansions prepared for them.

He came down in his glorified body to earth for a little while on a night which is peculiarly glorious in the New Testament. On the Mount of Transfiguration, to which the blessed Jesus had withdrawn with three of his disciples as he was approaching the death of the cross, Moses and Elijah appeared, bringing with them the atmosphere of heaven, and encircling the Redeemer in its radiance, and holding up his humanity in view of its awful trial.

Then Elijah went back to the beatific land. He has never since left it; but the spirit and power of his life and mission still go forth over the earth. It is the type and the inspiring principle of every preparatory work of repentance through which great triumphs of Jesus are introduced—the harbinger of the gospel in its rich redemption.

Such a story, in the simple telling or reading, without the form of moralizing upon it, should have a most persuasive influence.

It has been said that "the highest truth has been learned, not from a system, but a person, the God-man Christ Jesus—

> 'When truth in closest words shall fail,
> Then truth embodied in a tale
>   Will enter at the lowliest doors;
> And so the Word had breath, and wrought
>   With human hands the creed of creeds
>   In loveliness of perfect deeds,
>   More strong than all poetic thought.'" *

* " It is remarkable that Seneca acknowledges the need of a moral ideal—a pattern by which we can shape our conduct. He advises us to revolve the example of good men and heroes like Cato, in order to draw from them guidance, though he admits

Subordinate to that grand and divine life, every truly religious one pictured on the sacred pages has a similar influence; and none more nobly so than this of Elijah. It had its special place in the development of the sacred history. Those incidents of it which have been preserved by the inspired pen were selected because of the lessons that they should impress on succeeding ages. One series of these lessons is of special value in this scientific age, because

their imperfection and consequent insufficiency for this end. Christianity alone supplies this need by presenting human nature in its purity and perfection in the person of Christ."—Fisher's *Beginnings of Christianity*, p. 174.

The various meannesses which Homer attributes to his gods have led to the remark (Collins's *Homer*, p. 38) that "the conception of gods in human shape has always a tendency to monstrosities and caricature. How close, too, the supernatural and the grotesque seem to lie together may be seen even in the existing sculptures and carvings of ancient Christendom, and still more remarkably in the old miracle-plays, which mix buffoonery with the most sacred subjects in a manner which it is hard to reconcile with any real feeling of reverence." What an argument for Christianity and for the Bible lies in the contrast which is presented by the revealed and inspired delineation of *the* God incarnate!

of its connection with the permanent relation of God to the works of his hands.

(1.) The whole recorded history of Elijah manifests in a striking manner the control which God retains over the forces and operations of nature.

The doctrine which the Bible and true science unite in teaching is this: God created the universe in the beginning, and impressed upon it the laws under which it continues to exist and, in its various departments, to operate. According to those laws, the forces of nature move with that steady uniformity on which all human science is predicated and all human schemes are devised and carried out. But they are not free from the divine reins. The one great underlying force of the universe is the power of the Creator himself,

"Who, retired
Behind his own creation, works unseen
By the impure, and hears his word denied." *

* Dana, in his *Geology*, says (p. 604): "The method of evolu-

He will not lightly make any apparent break in the uniform rotation-march of the great machine. He will not so act as to destroy the confidence in the steady sequence of events with which he has endowed the human mind. But he does control all things. Nature is ruled in the interests of his great moral government, and so regally ruled that the bold assertion of a poet is not too sweeping, that

> " The course of nature is the art of God ;"

Or, as old Chaucer has it,

> " Nature, the vicare of the Almightie Lord."

He could, in extraordinary ways, influence and modify the operations of the tion admitted of abrupt transitions between species; but for the development of man there was required the special act of *a being above nature, whose supreme will is the source of natural law."*

And again, in the *American Journal of Science and Arts*, Oct., 1876, p. 251: " For the development of man, gifted with high reason and will, and thus made a power above nature, there was required, as Wallace has urged, a special act of a *Being above nature*, whose supreme will is not only the source of natural law, *but the working force of Nature herself."*

laws under which the works of his hands go on, as men can do in lower degrees; or, when he created, it was in his power so to provide that at the proper time there would appear to be extraordinary changes, though inwrought in the system from the beginning, which would advance his moral government. These would constitute miraculous interpositions of divine power. For the general object now had in view it matters little which of these two ideas of a miracle we adopt.

In the Bible history there were three periods when these demonstrations on the field of nature were bright and prominent.

First, in connection with the deliverance of God's chosen people from the bondage of Egypt, earth, air and water were all wonderfully alive beneath the direct power of the Most High, exerted through the potential voice and the potential rod of his accredited ambassadors, Moses and Aaron.

Fifteen centuries later, when the divine Redeemer came to earth to accomplish for men a greater deliverance, he brought down to Judea the sceptre with which from the heavenly throne he swayed the universe; and the Holy Land was thrilled by the energy with which he touched all the forces of nature and made them do his saving will.*

Almost midway between those two periods, when the land was cursed by the darkest and deepest apostasy from the national life to which the deliverance through Moses had introduced the people, and when a startling ministry of preparation for the greater deliverance by Jesus was needed, in the days of Elijah and Elisha the earth also

---

* "It is high time that oracular assertions of the impossibility of such exertions of power as the New Testament attributes to Christ, or of the impossibility of proving them under any circumstances, should be set aside. It is impertinent, on the ground of some metaphysical scheme—an *a priori* conception of the universe—to set these arbitrary limits to the power of spirit over nature. If a system of philosophy cannot find room for facts well attested by historical evidence, so much the worse for the philosophical system."—Fisher's *Beginnings of Christianity*, p. 462.

shook and the heavens glowed under the touches of God, which proved that nature was not a blind and inexorable deity, working on with unvarying tread, but that all her forces are under his immediate control.

Now, it is most significant that every act of Elijah which has been preserved in the inspired record is an exhibition of this relation in which God stands to his works. Of no one else, not even of Jesus, can this be said. Observe the facts:

Rain was withheld for three and a half years, and then fell upon the land according to the prophet's word. Most unnatural! Against the ordinary condition of the atmosphere! What would have come upon our modern observer if he had been on his watch-tower during those distressingly bright forty-two months? How monotonous and dreary would have been his report from day to day! "Higher barometer! Clear, dry, scorching weather! No change! What does it mean?" But God revealed to Elijah in advance the persistent dryness of the air, and then made known to him the day when clouds would appear and rain descend; and on the top of Carmel, while the sky continued to wear its brazen face, his boy kept looking, with the eye of faith in the prophet, and saw the first indication of the storm in the little cloud no bigger than a man's hand.

Irrational creatures were guided by the Lord in a strange manner to do his work of mercy. Ravens, influenced by him against the peculiarities of their nature, brought bread and flesh to the holy man day by day.

A woman in a heathen land, moved by a gracious influence upon her mind, against her natural promptings and with the failure of her scanty supply threatening her, took the prophet into her house and shared with him the little food which she had for herself and her boy; and as she did that, day by day and week by week for three years, the pitcher * and the cruse, against the course of nature, never became empty, but were kept supplied with meal and oil in a mysterious manner; and the boy, too, though he had died, was brought back to life in answer to the prophet's prayer.

On Mount Carmel preternatural fire, on the petition of Elijah, descended and consumed the burnt sacrifice and the wood and the stones and the dust, and licked up the water that was in the trench.

As he slept beneath the juniper tree an angel touched and awoke him, and he beheld a cake, on hot stones, made by no human baker, and a cruse of water placed at his head by no human agency; and, after a second sleep, he rose and ate and drank again, and then, in the strength of that bread and water, traveled for forty days.

On Mount Horeb a storm of wind, an

---

* The "barrel" of 1 Kings xvii. 12 is elsewhere translated "pitcher"—that is, an earthen jar.

earthquake, and a fire, that wrapped the barren, rocky region in flames, passed in quick succession before him—phenomena which, if at other times witnessed there in various degrees, yet brought about at that time and accompanied by the still small voice, showed that the Lord was passing by and sending them before him.

After the spoliation and murder of Naboth by Jezebel and Ahab the prophet denounced on the royal house strange and unlooked-for judgments, which exactly came upon them by remarkable combinations of natural events.

Because he was a man of God the fire came down from heaven upon two successive companies of soldiers who had been sent to capture him by violence.

The close of his earthly life was a suspension and overthrow of the great event which, under sin, comes to all, and which, certain scientists would make us believe, is a necessary step in the very evolution of matter and of life; for, against the law of gravity, he was borne aloft from the world, and, against the law of death, he lived and lives on for ever.

In all this there is thrown across the sacred page and out before the world a most splendid bracelet of history, every link of which is a miracle-diamond of the first water. The acts are facts of authentic history. They have in their support all the evidence, historical and moral, which sustains the Scripture as a revelation and an inspiration. We have far more certain proof for the truth of them than we have for the hypotheses which lie at the foundation of modern systems of knowledge. They are a stirring protest against what has been called the "dirt philosophy," which the teachers of an unscriptural and an irrational science inculcate, and which would make nature its own lord and master, without an overruling and all-pervading moral Being from whom it came. And they remind us that the God who then broke through his ordinary modes of procedure, and let his hand be seen and his voice be heard in those extraordinary dealings, still directs the forces of the universe as the expressions of his own will. "Nature is alive with a life received from God himself and mysteriously connected with him." *

(2.) A second truth that is most powerfully illustrated in this portion of the sacred history is, that God employs the forces of nature as agents for the punishment and chastisement of individuals and nations.

Drought and famine came upon Israel because of the sin against Jehovah into which Ahab had fallen and led the people.

Ahab went into a battle disguised, so that the soldiers of the Syrian king, who had given orders that his death alone should be striven after, could not recognize him;

---

* Shairp's *Poetic Interpretation of Nature*, p. 221.

but an "arrow shot at a venture" laid him low; and, carried back dead to Samaria, his blood was washed from his chariot in a particular place and licked up by the dogs of the city, because he had acted infamously toward a private Israelite; and the prophet had declared that exactly that death should meet him on account of that sin.

Ahaziah's accident and sickness terminated fatally because he had followed in the footsteps of his father and had contemned Jehovah.

Thus the power of the sun, by which the vapor is drawn from the seas and rivers and condensed into overshadowing clouds for rain; the course of an arrow from the bow of an unknown soldier and the instinct of irrational dogs; the effects of a fall and the working of a disease in the human body,— were controlled and directed by God for the infliction of his just judgments.

The Bible, from the beginning to the end, is full of proofs that the physical and the moral governments of God are intermingled and act and react upon each other.

As in man the soul affects the body and the body the soul, each suffering for the misdeeds or blest by the righteousness of the other; as the vices that weaken and undermine the body enervate the soul, which through the body influences and is influenced by the external world, while whatever strengthens the physical system has a tendency to clarify and give health to the mind; as the soul, educated and purified in holy habits, writes itself upon the face and with energy sweeps through the bodily frame:—so, in the wider sphere of the world and the universe, the sins of God's rational creatures jar the forces and operations of matter and react with suffering on the sinners; and holiness, to the extent to which it prevails, harmonizes and subdues and beneficently sways the mechanism of nature. God has established a connection between the two, and, whether by a pre-established harmony, or by his direct touches consistently with the laws which he impressed in the beginning, he deals with the one on account of the other.

Every period of great moral and religious excitement in the history of the world has exhibited this. The striking agitations and derangements and convulsions of nature with which prophecy surrounds the second coming of the Redeemer are pre-eminently suggestive of it.

All the forces of the universe are in God's hand, and he controls them as his agents to execute his judicial purposes. Even men can in a degree restrain and direct them. Much more can the almighty Creator and Judge.

As "we have, to a certain extent and in a certain way, power to suspend or counteract in individual cases the operation of a law of nature," so, and in a still higher and more sweeping degree, " by his intelligence and will God can bring into play a new cause which can suspend or counteract in a particular instance the usual working of a law of nature. That book, for example, would lie for ever where it is if no interference with the law of gravitation were possible; but I will to lift it, and the new cause, acting through my muscles upon the book, raises it notwithstanding gravitation. In the will of man, therefore, as operating first upon his own muscular nature, and second, through that upon external things, we have, in a certain sense and to a certain extent, a supernatural cause. But if the intelligence and will of man are equal to such interference with nature and nature's laws, can we deny to God a similar power? Or is it conceivable that he has formed in the universe a vast machine, and that he has deliberately shut himself out from all possibility of interfering with it for any purpose whatever, no matter how important? *

He did so judicially intervene in the

* *Presbyterian Quarterly*, vi. (new series), pp. 613, 614.

times of Elijah; and what he did then he does still. Let his direct touch be where it may, rain and drought, abundance and famine, health and sickness, storms and calms, commercial prosperity and commercial derangement and ruin, are not arbitrary events. They come under his providence; they are used as his judgments; his force directs them.

Our blessed Lord, however, in two of his utterances in the New Testament, guards against a rash construction of this fact, as a noted example in the Old Testament had also done. They both show that it is not safe for a finite mind dogmatically to make the application of this great law to particular cases, and upon it express a judgment as to the relative moral character of sufferers.

During the life of Jesus a tower was standing or going up in the city of Jerusalem near to the pool of Siloam. There were unskillful workmen then as there are now; bad builders; scaling contractors who would give the worst materials and the poorest workmanship for the greatest amount of the public money; peculators who would do public works and use the public funds in a way in which they would not employ their private means or their private buildings. And one day that tower fell and buried eighteen men in its ruins. A sudden judgment! Perhaps the careless master-builder was among the number, and deserved his fate. "But," cried out Jesus, "think ye that those eighteen were sinners above all the men that dwelt in Jerusalem? I tell you, nay; but except ye repent ye shall all likewise perish."

That remark followed another which the Lord had uttered in censure upon some busybodies of the day. The Jews were then in a very inflammable condition, and tumults among them were frequent. In a riotous disturbance that had taken place the troops of Pilate, the Roman governor, had massacred some Galileans while they were engaged in the temple-worship, and had mingled their blood with the blood of their sacrifices. Certain scandal-mongers came to the Master with the news, evidently supposing that particular crimes had brought upon the "slaughtered worshipers so hideous and tragical a fate." But the Divine One, sweeping aside their uncharitable judgment, declared: "Suppose ye that these Galileans were sinners above all the Galileans because they suffered such things? I tell you, nay; but except ye repent, ye shall all likewise perish."

With a heavy hand the Almighty had, long before that, come down on the three friends of Job because they attributed the severe chastisements, with which he had been visited, to secret, unknown, hypocritical sins.

The texture of society is so intricate, the various classes are so mixed together in this world, that the innocent are often involved with the guilty in the natural fruits of their deeds and in the judgments of God upon them. Hence, while it is prudent and wise for each to ask himself, when any trouble befalls him, Is this, may it be, for the correction of any errors of mine?—as the woman of Sarepta, when her boy died, called to mind her sinfulness of life—yet it is a usurpation of the exclusive right of the divine Judge for any mortal to pass such a judgment upon other sufferers.

In regard to nations there may be a greater sweep of human opinion. As a moral governor, God deals with them as well as with individuals. His sentences upon them take a longer time to work themselves out; but they are visited in their full extent in this world. In that respect nations differ from individuals, who pass into the future and meet the most tremendous part of their sentence there. But, in national inflictions especially, innocent individuals are swept along in the woes that are brought down by the guilty. Elijah himself, and the seven thousand who had never bowed the knee to Baal, suffered from the drought and famine which the sin of Ahab and of the mass of the nation drew upon the land.

Even in this, however, lies the germ of a practical thought for our guidance. No man liveth unto himself and no man dieth unto himself. We each influence and are influenced by others. A nation is made up of its individual members. Every one has something to do with shaping its character and course. Hence, as God deals with it for its general administration and for the sins which prevail, and as those who are exalted to office do so much to regulate that administration and to exalt or debase the public life, it is the duty of every one by influence and act to seek to purify both the people and their representative rulers. But it has largely come to pass in our cities and towns—though not to so great a degree in the rural regions—that the mass of the respectable, honest, conscientious men do not trouble themselves with the management of public affairs. They generally permit the primary elections of the parties to be held in places where no man of any self-respect can go. Those primary meetings practically settle the nominations in larger conventions. As a stream can rise no higher than its fountain, the nominees of such men cannot in general be expected to be better than themselves. Hence we have too often presented for office candidates between whom it is hard to choose. They make bad laws. They start extravagant enterprises in which robbery of the public money is practiced under politer names. They set bad examples, especially to the rising generation. They fearfully increase taxes. Then the respectable men who have not touched politics grow angry, and complain of their burdens and of the low class of public officials. But they suffer, and the poor suffer, and God is displeased with the immoralities which are practiced by public men and, under them, by the nation. Yet it is because the better classes attend exclusively to their private affairs, without remembering that they owe a duty to the public, to the state, to God. It is because they will tolerate in public matters a standard of morality which they would scorn to recognize and act upon in private affairs. It is because they do not insist that everywhere and at all times—in private business, in the management of fiduciary trusts and in civil government—the inflexible moral law of God shall be binding. That is largely the source of our troubles. We forget that a nation is a moral organism.

The last interview of Elijah with Ahab, in which the prophet foretold to the king his violent death and the disgraceful end of his whole family, was caused by the monarch's sin in making a false charge against Naboth, and thereby securing his murder, so as to get possession of his vineyard. On this Dean Stanley says: "It is the characteristic of the sacred history that the final doom of the dynasty of Omri should be called forth not by its idolatry, not by its persecution of the prophets, but by an act of injustice to an individual, a private citizen." This is too sweeping a remark. It needs qualification. For that act was the culmination of Ahab's long course of departure from the worship of the true God and of resistance to the divinely-sent prophets—the practical working out, in every-day life and in business-matters, of his violation of the theocratic law of the kingdom. It was the occasion, and one of the acts, which led to the passing of the death-sentence. But it *is* significant of the sanction which the revealed law throws around individual rights, of the jealous eye with which God looks at the dealings of rulers with the men whom they rule, of the care which he takes of those who cannot take care of themselves, and of the sternness with which he will visit the high and the powerful who dare to be arbitrary and unjust,—it is significant of all this that on such a sin as that the divine sentence was uttered. Those who despoil the widow and the orphan; those who grind the poor as between the upper and the nether millstone; those who make or administer laws in such a way that struggling men and women lose their homes and their means through their misfortune, not their fault; those who bring about a state of things which sell the houses from over the heads of the hardworking and the saving,—they may prosper for years, multiplying their gains, adding to their property, increasing their power. It may be difficult to track their movements; it may be impossible for human eyes to see where the fraud was practiced, and for human judgment to declare where the greatest guilt lies; but the God of heaven knows, and, as sure as he is just, judgment will be entailed upon the transgressors.

(3.) A third lesson, most powerfully exhibited in the story of Elijah, is that the sufferings which God inflicts through nature have in themselves no reclaiming power.

The three and a half years of drought and famine did not turn the Israelites—much less Ahab and Jezebel—from the worship of Baal. The judgment of fire upon the altar on Carmel and the destruction of the four hundred and fifty priests appeared to sweep the multitude into a renewed acknowledgment of Jehovah; but it was only a momentary enthusiasm, and Jezebel was hardened by the visitation. The passing of the sentence of death upon Ahab for his sin against Naboth made him rend his clothes and put sackcloth upon his flesh and fast and walk softly for a little while, so that he secured a temporary postponement of the full execution of the sentence; but, like a compressed spring, he quickly jumped up into his sinful course again, and went to his disgraceful death upon the battlefield. His death, and his son's death, and the knowledge of all that was denounced against the queen-wife and mother, did not soften her heart. She continued in her way, and, for years after Elijah's translation, went on in her God-defying, man-despising course, until, with her painted face and her tired head, she was thrown from the window of her palace in Jezreel, trampled under foot by Jehu's horse, her blood sprinkled on the wall and her carcass eaten by the dogs—as Elijah, seventeen years before, in Naboth's field, had predicted should come to pass.

Strange, was it not? in spite of all the plain denunciations from God, enforced as they were by one judgment after another, that through them Ahab for twelve years and Jezebel for twenty-nine years from Elijah's first appearance, persisted in their sinful rebellion and immorality, and that the people submitted to their tyranny and continued in their sin!

No, it was not strange. It was the legitimate working of simple human nature uninfluenced by the restraining and saving influence of the Holy Spirit.

In one of the paragraphs of his article on Lord Byron, Macaulay has — unintentionally, perhaps, but most powerfully — described the searing influence of afflictions in themselves. With great genius and much to build him up, Byron lived from the first in an atmosphere loaded with pains and aggravations in body and in mind; and under their influence, "year after year and month after month, he continued to repeat that to be wretched is the destiny of all; that to be eminently wretched is the destiny of the eminent; that all the desires by which we are cursed lead alike to misery; if they are not gratified, to the misery of disappointment; if they are gratified, to the misery of satiety. His heroes are men who have arrived by different roads at the same goal of despair, who are sick of life, who are at war with society, who are supported in their anguish only by an unconquerable pride resembling that of Prometheus on the rock or of Satan in the burning marl; who can master their agonies by the force of their will; and who to the last defy the whole power of earth and heaven. He always described himself as a man of the same kind with his favored creatures—as a man whose heart had been withered, whose capacity for happiness was gone and could not be restored, but whose invincible spirit dared the worst that could befall him here or hereafter."

That was—that is—hell. And it is a state which does not burn out or purify itself. Once beyond the grace of God—which is withdrawn from the unsaved at death—it is unending.

The inefficacy of wrathful judgments to save was one great lesson which was taught by God's manifestation of himself to Elijah on Horeb. The prophet was disheartened because the result of the trial on Carmel had not converted Jezebel, or at least rallied the people to his support against her; but that, on the contrary, upon the very day when it took place, and while the land was rejoicing in the rain which had come according to his word, she threatened him with death, and the people failed him and left him alone. His nature was of the vindicatory,* judicial, stern cast, jealous for God and his law; though he was not wanting in tenderness. But Jehovah showed him that the real power for the good of men, his effectual influence for their salvation, was not in the earthquake, the wind, the fire, which blast and destroy the face of nature, but in the gentle influence which enters the heart and sweetly constrains it to follow him. The other — the severe — dealings of his judgment and wrath may startle, attract attention, produce fear for a time: to save, the still small voice must follow them.

* Not "vindictive;" there is a difference in the meaning of the two words.

The ministry of Elijah seems to be made prominent in the sacred history, especially in contrast with that of Elisha, his successor, and still more in contrast with that of Jesus, to burn this lesson into the mind and heart of the Church of God. "Not in his own mission, grand and gigantic as it was, would after ages so clearly discern the divine inspiration as in the still small voice of justice that breathed through the writings of the later prophets, for whom he only prepared the way—Hosea, Amos, Micah, Isaiah, Jeremiah. Not in the vengeance which through Hazael and Jehu was to sweep away the house of Omri, so much as in the discerning love which was to spare the seven thousand; not in the strong east wind that parted the Red Sea, or the fire that swept the top of Sinai, or the earthquake that shook down the walls of Jericho, would God be brought so near to man as in the ministrations of Him whose cry was not heard in the streets; in the awful stillness of the cross; in the never-failing order of providence; in the silent, insensible influence of good deeds and good words, of God and of man. This is the predictive element of Elijah's prophecies. This is the sign that the history of the Church had made a vast stride since the days of Moses. Here we see in an irresistible form the true unity of the Bible. The sacred narrative rises above itself to a world hidden as yet from the view of those to whom the vision was revealed. There is already a Gospel of Elijah." *

---

* Stanley's *History of the Jewish Church*, ii., pp. 343, 344.

The dean is not so admirable when he adds: " He, the farthest removed of all the prophets from the evangelical spirit and character, has yet enshrined in the heart of his story *the most forcible of all protests against the hardness of Judaism*, the noblest anticipation of the breadth and depth of Christianity." A great many errors of the so-called liberal and broad Church writers of the day, and of the more pronounced rejecters of the Old Testament, would be avoided if they were to discriminate carefully between Judaism as revealed by God and as perverted, distorted, imperfectly exhibited, by those who professed it; between the pure revelation itself and its corruptions among the men who had it; between the truths really taught by Moses and the prophets on

One incident in the earthly life of our blessed Redeemer very vividly brings out the contrast between his mission and that of the prophet. The people of a certain Samaritan village denied him their hospitality because he was going up to Jerusalem. James and John thereupon said to him, "Lord, wilt thou that we command fire to come down from heaven and consume them, even as Elias did? But he turned and rebuked them and said, Ye know not what manner of spirit ye are of. For the Son of man is not come to destroy men's lives, but to save them." Luke ix. 53-56.

The judicial acts of wrath which Elijah

the one hand, and the traditions of the elders and the narrowing conduct of the later Jews generally on the other. So, too, when Stanley, speaking of the Horeb scene, says (p. 340), "It was a marked crisis not only in his own life, but in the history of the whole prophetic dispensation," we can go with him. But the Scriptures do not justify his assertion that "it was, if not the first prophetic call to Elijah, the first prophetic manifestation to him of the divine Will and the divine Nature." Such a manifestation the Tishbite certainly had in the very first incident of his life that is made known to us.

7

wrought were not wrong. They were required by the condition of the nation and the age. They had their place in the development of God's moral government. Otherwise Elijah would not have been honored by God as he was.

But the Redeemer's life and mission, for which the fiery Elijah and Elijah's antitype prepared the way, were of a different cast. He did no work of death to men. None of his miracles, except that of the blasting of the fig tree, were acts of destruction. Kindness, beneficence, mercy, clothed them all. He went about doing good. Along the highways and the byways, through the streets and into the homes of Judea, he scattered blessings with the profusion of an almighty Monarch. And the prevalent tone of his ministry was found in the winning words and the persuasive invitations with which he sought to bring the weary and heavy-laden to himself: "I am come to seek and save the lost."

None of his followers are now authorized to call down fire, to use force, to compel men to receive him; nor may they deal harshly with those who refuse to yield to his sceptre. They who have done this knew not what manner of spirit they were of. His ministry was kindness: by kindness alone may his followers seek to overcome his enemies and rejecters.

With this, as glowing in the brighter relief and in richer tints of loveliness and magnificence, because of the contrast with the storms, the earthquakes, the fires of Elijah's ministry, I close the exhibition of this series of lessons.

The loving ministry of Jesus on earth, and, following that, the still, small, but powerful, ministry of the Spirit in the soul; the pure and perfect life of the God-man which quietly marked the way to heaven; the sacrificial death which closed the road to perdition and opened the celestial gates; the tender power which did not break the bruised reed nor quench the smoking flax; the divine voice that roars not through a storm-cloud, and strikes not in the lightning, and speaks not in violence, but which steals into the heart and enlightens the conscience and binds the soul as with the cords of a man; the gospel of the atoning Son of God who came into the world not to condemn the world, but that the world through him might be saved,—this is the redeeming and regenerating power that bends from the throne of heaven to earth, and draws the saved world up within the charmed circle of the rainbow which in reflected brightness surrounds the Most High.

Behold it with admiration and with gratitude! Behold the Lamb of God which taketh away the sin of the world. The Lamb, meek, quiet, suffering, sacrificial! Not smiting, but dying; not calling down fire from heaven, but baring his own bosom to the storm-cloud; not compelling, but winning; not taking our life, but giving his own!

Behold the richness and the glory of his redemption: from hell and from sin; in time and for eternity.

Behold the love-scene and the love-gift; and, as you behold, submit to its almighty influence, and, floating upon it, move on heavenward.

"Herein is love; not that we loved God, but that he loved us and sent his Son to die for us."

III.

GOD'S WORK, AND HIS AGENTS.

THE conflict of fire on Mount Carmel between Elijah the prophet of Jehovah and the four hundred and fifty prophets of Baal excited the Israelitish multitude to a clamorous recognition of the covenant God of their nation, and led them, under Elijah's lead, to inflict deserved death upon the foreign and treasonous idolaters. It was immediately followed, too, in response to Elijah's prayer and in accordance with his assertion, by a great rain which broke the three and a half years' drought. The two events combined — the judgment and the mercy — may have touched the heart of King Ahab.

But Queen Jezebel had not been on the mount when the fire of God descended upon it. She came not under the influence of an immediate contact with the wonder. Like a modern scientific skeptic, she could explain the happening of the rain by purely natural laws, and could account for the prophet's promise of it by saying that he had detected changes in the atmosphere which gave a premonition of it, and he just happened to tell the time when it was to come. Therefore, when Ahab, dripping wet and agitated by the news which he had of the astonishing spiritual duel and of the execution of the four hundred and fifty priests, reached the palace in Jezreel, an angry passion inflamed her. Her stony mind was not melted by the fire of God. Her dry, arid, baked heart was not softened by the copious rain which was such a blessing to the land. She thought more of the terrific blow that her false religion had received than of the apparent return of the true

God to his people. Unsubdued by the suffering through which the nation had passed, unconvinced by the manner in which Jehovah had spoken from heaven, fiercely mad toward the man whom the Most High had used as his messenger of wrath and of mercy, she sent to Elijah the message: "So let the gods do to me, and more also, if I make not thy life as the life of one of them by to-morrow about this time."

It is not likely that, while the people were excited and enthusiastic over the day's occurrence, she could have carried out that threat.

It may be that she hoped the report of her declaration would frighten Elijah and lead him to fly, and so put in peril the fruits of his victory.

More probably the threat was the hasty utterance of an angry woman carried away by her passion, and having as yet no definite idea of what she could do or intended to do, or of the effect which her message would have.

But it did frighten the bold prophet; and that very night, without stopping to see whether the queen would attempt to carry her threat into effect, or whether the people would not stand between him and her, he arose and went for his life.

Accompanied by no one but his servant, he hastened from the dominions of Ahab to Beersheba in Judah. But not there did he feel himself to be safe, for the king of Judah was married to a daughter of Ahab and Jezebel. Therefore, leaving his servant, he hastened on alone a day's journey into the wilderness, and took his first rest beneath a juniper or broom tree. And there he sat down with only one desire—that he might be permitted to die.

"It is enough; now, O Lord, take away my life: for I am not better than my fathers."

Behold the unsuccessful, discouraged, broken-hearted man, tired of life, asking for death as a blessing!

Can it be? Is this the bold prophet who, three and a half years before, faced the despotic king in his palace and told him that for his sins and the sins of the people the land was to be cursed? Is this the intercessor with God whose prayer had opened and closed heaven, withheld and brought rain? Is this the outspoken preacher who not many hours before had said to the king, when he tried to overawe him, "Thou art the troubler of Israel"? Is this Jehovah's unfaltering worshiper who had the faith and the courage to challenge the whole host of Baal-worshipers to the deciding contest on Carmel? Is this the same man? Yes, the same. "The strong man, weak as a child, bent under the burden of unspeakable misery. Like some great eagle who has soared aloft on sublime wings, but when nearest the sun, smitten by a secret shaft, falls like a thunderbolt, and we gaze sadly on the clear eye dimmed over with the dust of earth, and on the confused wreck of mighty pinions, so deep is the fall, so low the strength, of him who had triumphed on Carmel."

What had produced this transformation? How are this weakness and this apparent want of faith to be accounted for?

The change and lapse are not to be wondered at. Elijah was a man of like passions with ourselves. A knowledge of the human nature which we all wear explains his condition under the juniper tree.

Some think that he had been carried into the execution of the four hundred and fifty priests of Baal by an excess of zeal, and that, not having had the authority of God for the act, his conscience condemned him, and produced first the fear which caused him to run from Jezebel, and then the depression of spirits which made him feel that his mission was a failure and that death would be preferable to life. He was conscience-smitten, and therefore weak.

This view I do not entertain for one moment.

Others think that the prophet was disappointed because the people did not rally to his support against the queen; that he had been exulting too much in his work, and was thus left to himself that he might be humbled; and that this was brought about by a natural reaction in his physical system which left him mentally prostrated.

The last idea of this statement contains, I think, a full explanation. Elijah did not wait to see whether the people would stand up for him and for God against the foreign queen. I cannot perceive in his response to the Lord on Mount Horeb any tone of undue egotism. Carried away by a sudden panic on the very night of his triumph, as soon as he heard of the threat of Jezebel, he fled from Jezreel; and his fear was followed by deep despondency of spirit, despair, sense of utter failure in his mission; and both the fear and the despondency dragged him down because his physical system had been prostrated by what he had passed through.

"Morbid melancholy generally succeeds morbid excitement." The mutual influence of the mind and the body upon each other is such that a protracted and undue tension of either unstrings the other. A diseased or exhausted physical system is sure to tell upon mental exercises. Nervous prostration will bring with it spiritual dullness.

Now look at what Elijah had suffered. For three years he had been in a foreign land, living from hand to mouth on short allowance. That was immediately followed by the tremendous conflict of Mount Carmel through that long day on which the priests of Baal were vainly calling for fire to consume their sacrifice, and at the close of which Elijah poured out the energy of his soul in his petition to Jehovah. Then the season of suffering banishment and the day of exhausting struggle were closed by his run of ten or twelve miles from Carmel to

Jezreel beside the royal chariot, he keeping up with it, too, until the city was reached. All that was enough to weaken the man bodily. His mental agitation must have shed over his physical nature an exciting glow which could not but lead to a reaction. The threat of Jezebel found him a tired-out man. Looking through the exhausted body upon the external world, the mind could not see things in their normal light. The strong man was broken down into the feebleness of a child. His intellect was gloomily clouded. His feelings were depressed.

The history of the Church and of the world is full of similar cases. Many a strong man, after excessive toil and anxiety and emotional excitement, has been found mentally more helpless than a babe, and spiritually shrouded with the blackest despair. Many a hero after a great triumph in which others thought he was in every way successful, has, in the retirement of his own home, been bemoaning his failure. Even the Redeemer was prophetically represented as saying, "I have labored in vain, I have spent my strength for naught and in vain," though his divine power enabled him immediately to add: "Surely my judgment is with the Lord, and my work [or my reward] with my God." Isa. xlix. 4.

Elijah, then, under the juniper tree is a physically exhausted man; and his depressed condition of body has thrown a darkness over his mind and made him feel so discouraged that he would rather die than live. He was far more excusable than was Moses when he offered a similar prayer: "If thou deal thus with me, kill me, I pray thee, out of hand, if I have found favor in thy sight, and let me not see my wretchedness;" or than Jonah, who, displeased and angry because God announced his mercy toward Nineveh, cried out: "Therefore now, O Lord, take, I beseech thee, my life from me, for it is better for me to die than to live."

It is very interesting to observe how the divine Physician dealt with the prophet when he was found in that weak state.

First of all, he strengthened his body by subduing him into sleep and nourishing him with food. "So he giveth his beloved sleep"—"tired nature's sweet restorer, balmy sleep." Thus the physical and mental excitement of the man was calmed, and new fuel was given to the furnace which keeps up the life of the body.

Then he took him away to one of the grandest and wildest scenes of nature, and there by a remarkable manifestation taught him that the kind of work which he had been commissioned to perform was a startling and preparatory one, and that he must not expect to accomplish everything and at once. His mission was largely punitive, but all that it could do was to awaken, to startle, to make anxious; following that, a still, gentle influence of the Spirit must do the really saving work.

It is not to be overlooked that in connection with this special and revealing power of God there was a natural influence exerted upon the mind of the prophet. Direct contact with nature is a great means of instruction and of strength for the mind. It is good for everybody occasionally to get away from bricks and mortar, from crowded streets and active work, even from rural spots that have undergone a high artificial cultivation, and, in some of nature's milder or some of her grander scenes, look quietly upon her and get into communion with her. It makes a man the better able to go back to his daily employment. Change of scene helps the mind. It had that influence on Elijah. In a lower degree, the pastor who leaves his place after a season of hard labor, and spends some weeks in rural retirement or on a mountain-height, is not wasting his time, but strengthening himself the better for his future work.

Following that, God showed the prophet

that the true cause was not at so low an ebb as he in his despondency thought it was. He was not alone in the service of Jehovah. Seven thousand Israelites had continued faithful; not a large number, it was true, but still better than he thought. Things are generally more favorable than men in their desponding moods imagine.

The Lord also provided a companion and a helper for his servant in the future. Hitherto he had been a solitary man—alone in his work. Alone! alone! alone! he declares on three different occasions. And a man who has not some very close friend to whom he may freely unbosom himself, and from whom he may receive sympathy in sorrow and appreciation in success, is really in a very weak condition. Hence, from that time forward, after this revelation of weakness in Elijah, Elisha became his constant companion.

Then, to crown the whole, God refused to answer the prayer for a solitary death under the juniper tree—"O Lord, take away my life." But the Lord had something more glorious for him than such an obscure end. The translation by a whirlwind into heaven ten years later was better and grander. The Lord does not answer all the petitions of his people as they present them. What a blessing it is that he does not! For they often ask what they think would be a good, as in his state of mind Elijah thought death would be a good to him; but God refuses because he has for them something better. Involved in the efficacy of prayer is the recognition of God as knowing the best way to answer.

The great prophet does not seem ever to have fallen again into a desponding frame of mind. He came forth from that episode in his history strengthened, and was always afterward himself as the grace of God had made him. But the effects of his temporary lapse remained. And there are three grand permanent lessons which may be derived from the episode.

(1.) Behold an illustration of the way in which God sometimes permits breaks in the progress of his work.

At the close of the fire-contest on Carmel how favorable everything appeared to be for a revolution which would have swept the heathen Jezebel from the throne and reestablished the worship of Jehovah in its purity! The people were excited. They had been compelled to cry out, "Jehovah, he is God! Jehovah, he is God!" All that was needed was a leader to stimulate and direct them; for great leaders are needed in the world and in the Church—men of intellect; men of education; men of courage; men who dare to resist the wrong, to run against the multitude when they are misled, to guide them when they are aroused to a desire to do right, to burst the shackles of party when the hacks of the party show that they would sacrifice the public good rather than lose their influence and emoluments, to rise above a temporary clamor and do what their consciences tell them is right, even though for a time it be under a cloud. Such men are needed. The masses cannot do much without them.

All party-men do not believe this. I remember a conversation which I had a few years ago with an excellent young man who belonged to the class of politicians that have a good deal to do with party machinery. Just at that time the most of the leaders of the organization to which he belonged were trying to force it into a measure which, it was afterward seen, would have been suicidal. Some of the very able men of the party, however, strove against it and prevented it. They were men of fine intellect, strong will, and unimpeachable moral character. My friend, referring to them with great disapprobation because they were running against the will of the smaller lights, said bitterly that he believed great men were really a curse to a country! A curse — because, with their clear mind seeing the inevitable results of the proposed procedure, and with their strong will daring to resist what they believed to be wrong, and with their influence swaying the people finally to their side! A curse—because the little, selfish, narrow-minded men could not rule. Ah! may God continue to curse us, as he has done hitherto at critical emergencies, with such men, and keep our people "amenable to that control to which it is the glory of free nations to submit themselves—the control of superior minds"!*

It is very true that history is largely made up of the bad actions of extraordinary men; that the most noted destroyers and deceivers of our species, all the founders of arbitrary governments and false religions, were extraordinary men; and that nine-tenths of the calamities which have befallen the human race had their origin in the union of high intelligence with low desires.† But

---
* Macaulay's *Hist. of England*, viii., p. 131.
† Macaulay's "Essay on Bacon."

when God raises up, in the Church or in the state, men of great mind and noble heart as leaders, he gives the people one of the greatest blessings. Generally circumstances fashion them, and they in turn fashion circumstances as the car of progress needs them. "The real rulers of our world are few in any community or under any form of government. They are always dangerous when there is a low degree of virtue or intelligence among those whom they represent. Certain it is that their power is nearly absolute when they are sustained by passion or prejudice. . . . The liberties of Rome were not overturned by fanatical rulers, but by those who availed themselves of the passions which they themselves did not feel, in order to compass their selfish ends. And that is the great danger in republics—that bad men rise by the suffrage of foolish people, whom they deceive by affecting to fall in with their wishes." *

* Lord's *Old Roman World*, p. 216.

But if a great leader fails when he is most needed, what a public calamity it is!

And just at the critical moment Elijah failed! He abandoned his post. When he ought to have been in Samaria or Jezreel restoring the true religion, he was in Arabia, censured by God with the question, "What doest thou here, Elijah?" Jezebel continued for years to have her own way. When Elijah reappeared he was not able to catch up the dropped thread of his work. The strength of the man who ought to have drawn the ark forward and upward gave out, and the ark retrograded.

The Almighty does his work on earth through human instruments, and the most important of human instruments sometimes sadly break.

Yet behind this is an important fact which was symbolized in the Horeb revelation. God does not move his Church and his cause forward through the passionate excitement of men. He uses the enlightened reason, judgment, conscience, for its real development and advancement. The Israelites had been excited by the Carmel conflict, but that was not sufficient: another kind of training was needed to restore them; and that was a matter of time.

"The method of providence in history is never magical. In proportion to the magnitude of the catastrophe are the length of time and the variety of agencies which are employed in producing it." *

God permitted four thousand years to pass after the Fall and after the promise of the Redeemer before the Saviour appeared on the earth. Through all that period a necessary though slow work of preparation was in progress among the Gentiles and among the Jews. Nearly nineteen hundred years have passed, and yet immense tracts of the world have not been touched by Christianity.

Very slow—very slow indeed—to human

* Fisher's *History of the Reformation.*

eyes appears to be the course of the Church of God. But progress it makes, though sometimes, if you look only at little segments of it, there might appear to be none.

What a brilliant historian has said of his country is pre-eminently true of the history of the religion of Jesus. Its progress resembles the motion of the sea when the tide is rising: "Each successive wave rushes forward, breaks and rolls back, but the great flood is steadily coming in. A person who looked on the waters only for a moment might fancy that they were retiring. A person who looked on them only for five minutes might fancy that they were rushing capriciously to and fro. But when he keeps his eye on them for a quarter of an hour, and sees one sea-mark disappear after another, it is impossible for him to doubt of the general direction in which the ocean is moving." Not in a straight line, but by advancing orbits is the course of history.

God did not use the great and exciting day's contest on Carmel to make a sudden and long stride for his religion. One lesson from this, for all ages, is that force and animal and emotional excitement are not the agencies that he employs for the spread of true spirituality. The only instrumentality that he owns is the truth—the efficient power, that of the Holy Spirit. We may resort to other means to hasten his work, but in the real accomplishment of it they will fail. By various theatrical appliances a congregation may be stirred up and fired to a fever-heat, and, under the artificial high-pressure, numerous conversions may be reported. But all that may only burn over the neighborhood, and, in the end, hurt religion in the way in which the world looks at it. The real work is done only by the Spirit, through the instrumentality of the truth plainly presented. Sometimes in the Church at large, or in a particular congregation, we may think it moves not rapidly enough; but the sovereignty is God's in the extent to which he will make it successful.

(2.) Behold in Elijah an illustration of the apparent failure on the part of a great man in doing the work to which the Lord had called him.

When he asked God to let him die, he felt that he had been unsuccessful. And from his own point of view and that of his contemporaries such was the case.

More than that, his subsequent ministry must have been looked upon in the same light. His mission was that of a warfare against the vicious irreligion which sat upon the throne and prevailed through the nation of Israel. But when he was taken from the earth, that religion still existed and reigned, and seemed to have lost none of its power. Jezebel, whose threat drove the prophet from the kingdom at the moment when victory seemed to be in his grasp, lived for about fourteen years after he disappeared from the earth; and to the last her influence was felt in Israel, and in Judah also. No doubt her minions were often in the habit of talking about the unavailing struggles which the rough-looking man of God had made against her and against her religion.

To the world the life of Elijah seemed to be a wretched failure. He left his nation as he found it at the commencement of his ministry—sunk in irreligion and vice. For thirteen or fourteen years he struggled against the current of his day and people: an earnest man of prayer; a strict worshiper of the Most High; a preacher of righteousness in conflict with the corruption that prevailed in high places and in low; a worker of miracles which could not but startle the people: and yet he disappeared at the end, with only one personal attendant in his company, with a few students in the schools of the prophets watching his course from a distance, with no following among the people—the seven thousand who may have remained in heart and in life faithful to Jehovah making no move under his lead to rid themselves of the debauching heathen religion,

Did not his great antitype, John the Baptist, appear to be as great a failure? For a little while the multitude hung upon his burning words of rude and stern eloquence and submitted to his baptism; but on the clamor of a vile woman, who had been offended by his faithfulness, he was murdered in a prison, and his head was carried, as a dainty morsel, on a plate to the room of the lewd conspirators against his life. Moreover, the words which he preached and the work that he wrought placed no permanent obstacle in the career of sin down which the Jewish nation was running. Nor did they prepare the hearts of many for the reception of Jesus. Only two or three of his disciples, guided by him, became the devoted followers of the Redeemer, and, as his apostles, helped to extend his Church.

The life of Jesus himself—what a failure that appeared to be to the men of his day, especially to his enemies who put him to death! In spite of his pure and holy life, his beautiful and inspiring words, his miraculous and beneficent deeds, he was nailed to the cross, no hand being raised to deliver him, no voice heard to cry out shame on the horrid murder when Pilate, through the importunity of the priests, passed the sentence of death upon him. Think you that the Scribes and Pharisees, hypocrites who hated him because his instructions were a sweeping condemnation of their teachings and lives, did not on the night of his crucifixion consider that he had met with a disgraceful defeat?

But did he really fail? Nay, verily. "From that very hour of defeat and death there went forth the world's life—from that very moment of apparent failure there proceeded forth into the ages the spirit of the conquering cross." The death itself was a triumph over death; and the divine words which were uttered during the short life that preceded it have gone forth conquering and to conquer, from soul to soul and from nation to nation.

And Elijah—the very thing that God revealed to him in the vision of Horeb was that his work should proceed—that it should not cease with his disappearance from earth, but that Hazael and Jehu and Elisha, prepared by him, would do it successfully. Ever since, too, his example and his spirit have been abroad in the world, protesting against sin and preparing the way for the Messiah.

Jezebel gloated over the prophet as a conquered man; God, by translating him, pronounced him a man without a peer on earth and in heaven.

Many a great man has, like him, seemed to himself and to his own generation to have been unsuccessful; and so many a man of smaller mind, but large and consecrated heart, in a lower position, has been looked upon by his little world. But in the kingdom of heaven success will be written against the name and all over the life.

More than two centuries ago the English nation rose in rebellion against Charles I., one of the meanest of their monarchs; and beneath the lead of some of the truest of patriots established a better government, which, under the guidance of Cromwell, though perverted in some of its essential elements, made the country a power in the earth. But a reaction took place after the death of Oliver. The debased son of the faithless monarch was restored. Contempt was poured upon the names and the remains of the Parliamentary leaders who had overthrown the king. The body of Cromwell was taken from its grave and hung upon a scaffold. "All London crowded to shout and laugh around the gibbet where hung the rotting remains of a prince who had made England the dread of the world; who had been the chief founder of her maritime greatness and of her colonial empire; who had conquered Scotland and Ireland; who had humbled Holland and Spain; the terror of whose name had been as a guard around every English traveler in remote countries and around every Protestant congregation in the hearts of Catholic empires."*

But was the work of that generation of stout-hearted, hard-headed, blow-dealing Puritans really lost? Nay: its principles reappeared in a purer form in the Revolution of 1688, and higher and purer still in the American Revolution of 1776; and have ever since been leavening the nations with true liberty, law and order.

A brilliant preacher has said, perhaps with a tinge of exaggeration caused by his own personal feelings, that "man is to de-

* Macaulay's *England*, iii., p. 289.

sire success; but success rarely comes. The wisest has written upon life, 'All is vanity'—that is, nothingness. The tradesman sees the noble fortune for which he lived, every coin of which is the representative of so much time and labor spent, squandered by a spendthrift son. The purest statesmen find themselves at last neglected and rewarded by defeat. Almost never can a man look back on life and say that its anticipations have been realized. For the most part, life is a disappointment, and the moments in which this is keenly realized are moments like those of Elijah." *

But, after all, "in God's world, for those that are in earnest, there is no real failure. No work truly done, no word earnestly spoken, no sacrifice freely made, was ever made in vain." The apparent success, to the eye of man, may not be immediate, but it works on in circles widening for ever and ever.

* F. W. Robertson.

There is an apparent, a superficial, a fleeting success which may be commanded very hastily by the most ordinary minds— like the effervescence of a fermenting liquor which is really poisonous. This may be enjoyed by a shrewd, heartless and dishonest business-man who will do anything to make a dollar, and will hoard it when made. It may be organized by the politician who will pander to party managers and believe in men more than principles. It may be sensationalized by a minister and a church who will depend on something else than the earnest exhibition of the truth and the scriptural worship of God to gather and to hold a congregation; for there are multitudes of people who, unused to real, scriptural, thoughtful, preaching and accustomed to wild ranting and waves of physical emotion, are like the boy in *The Heart of Midlothian*, who pushed away the lady's guineas with contempt and insisted on having white money—preferring the silver with which he was familiar, and which was constantly passing about from hand to hand, to the gold which he had never before seen and with the value of which he was unacquainted.

When a man is blessed with immediate and manifest success in his business or profession, or in some work for God, it is very pleasant and exhilarating and to be acknowledged with gratitude. But when success is delayed or withheld, the words of a thoughtful writer may be comforting: "I confess that increasing years bring with them an increasing respect for men who do not succeed in life, as these words are commonly used. Ill-success sometimes arises from a conscience too sensitive, a taste too fastidious, a self-forgetfulness too romantic, a modesty too retiring. I will not go so far as to say with a living poet that the world knows nothing of its greatest men; but there are forms of greatness, or at least of excellence, which die and make no sign; there are martyrs that miss the palm, but not the stake; heroes without the laurel, and conquerors without the triumph."

But oftentimes "apparent defeat is real victory, and there is a heaven for those who have nobly and truly failed on earth."*

"Well done"—not *successful*, but—"*good* and *faithful* servant!" will be the rewarding judgment by the great Judge.

(3.) Behold in God's treatment of Elijah an illustration of the tenderness with which he deals with his people when depressed and sad because apparently failing.

He did not reprove the prophet for that weakness and despondency, and for that impatient prayer, which were the result of an overwrought and overstrung physical system; though, when strength was regained, he did tenderly rebuke him for his absence from his post by the question, "What doest thou here, Elijah?"

* F. W. Robertson.

As beneath the juniper tree the Lord soothed him into a refreshing slumber and furnished him with needed food, and then kindly corrected his error, so all through his life he kept him under his protection. He commanded the ravens to feed him. He put it into the heart of the woman of Sarepta to share her scanty supply with him. He provided a faithful companion for him. And then he translated him to the ineffable glory and bliss of his presence in heaven.

A bruised reed the Divine One will not break, and a smoking flax will he not quench. Many a dull state spiritually is due to an unstrung system physically; and the Redeemer looks upon it with a tender and compassionate eye.

Moreover, he always provides for his people who are faithful—whether in high or low positions—in different ways from that in which he looked after Elijah, but yet as really. He does not always give them what they would like and as they would like it. He does not always make them successful according to their own preconceived idea. Elijah was sometimes in difficult straits—dependent on ravens! on a poor widow! But provided for, and at last gloriously rewarded! So God still permits many of his people to suffer much and to want many things. But he watches over them all most tenderly; and when their work is over he takes them to the land of full deliverance. "The world will support you when you have constrained its votes by a manifestation of power, and shrink from you when power and greatness are no longer on your side." But so will not God do.

After all, which was the better and happier life—that of the pampered Ahab and Jezebel in the ivory palace of Samaria and the country-seat of Jezreel, with all that wealth could provide, and then their death of infamy and an abode in hell; or the coarser life of Elijah, with his scanty fare at times, but then his bright translation and the unfailing glory of his heavenly abode?

Christian, whether suffering or rejoicing, in want or in abundance, exhilarated in soul or despondent, hold on to your faith in God and patiently persevere in your daily life, though it may be obscure; do honestly and conscientiously your work for others and for God in the station in which he has placed you; keep on at it in spite of apparent defeat, want of success, discouragement, failure of heart and skeptical questioning of soul; live and labor on in the fear of God until he sends his angel to bear your soul aloft to the glory in which bask all his glorified people.

IV.
THE CHURCH AND IMMORTALITY.

FEW beautifully-variegated pieces of glass in the kaleidoscope form, by the rotation of the instrument, an almost endless succession of richly-colored pictures. New arrangements and new combinations are made by every turn, but the pieces behind the glass and within the tube are few in number and in themselves quite insignificant.

Like to this is the exhibition which may be made of the biographical and historical facts that have been preserved in the Bible. Nowhere else do we find such careful condensation and selection of incidents. Very small in number are the acts and the words of any of the great scriptural characters who have thus been embalmed. Some of the facts might appear in themselves to be trivial, while others are of manifest and far-reaching importance; but all are selected because of some general truth to be learned from them in future ages. Never do they lose their freshness of interest. The man who has read them year after year, scores of times, sees new beauties and new applications in them on every perusal. The more he meditates upon them, the greater and the more widespread are the lessons they teach. It is not with them as Plutarch tells us it was with the defence which a lawyer, Lysias, wrote for a man who was to be tried by one of the Athenian tribunals. The speech was written by the lawyer, to be committed to memory by the defendant and delivered by him in court. "Long before the defendant had learned the speech by heart he became so much dissatisfied with it that he went in great distress to the author. 'I was delighted with your speech the first time I read it; but I liked it less the second time, and still less the third time; and now it seems to me to be no defence at all.'—'My good friend,' said Lysias, 'you quite forget that the judges are to hear it only once.'" But the force and beauty and application of these scriptural narratives do not vanish on a reperusal, as does the value of many merely human compositions. They are capable of almost endless combinations and applications in the general light of the Bible and by the turning touch of a thoughtful mind.

In a pre-eminent degree does this remark apply to the life of Elijah. Very few of the acts and words which made up his twelve or fourteen years' ministry have been preserved. We can quickly count them on our fingers. But when we place them under the full light of God's Word and revolve them in the mind, they make one gorgeous picture after another, and on all sides burst forth flashes of light which strike human nature in numerous relations. A superficial person may think that the facts are soon grasped and sounded. But series after series of lessons shoot up with every turn of the instrument and upon every glance of the eye. The same facts appear and reappear in every view—the same, yet different.

A special New Testament turn of the kaleidoscope will arrange these facts of Elijah's life in a threefold combination, and illustrate (1) God's preservation of his Church; (2) his wide love and the true catholicity of his Church; (3) the exhilarating views of the future under which his people have always lived. These are the three great points to confirm which the New Testament appeals to this portion of the ancient history.

(1.) God has always preserved for himself in the world a true people. The Church is indestructible.

The apostle Paul, in Romans xi 2-4, exclaims: "Wot ye not what the Scripture saith of Elias? How he maketh intercession to God against Israel, saying, Lord, they have killed thy prophets and digged down thine altars; and I am left alone, and they seek my life? But what saith the answer of God to him? I have reserved to myself seven thousand men who have not bowed the knee to Baal."

Recall again the circumstances to which the apostle refers. Elijah had triumphed over the priests of Baal on Carmel. But, overcome by fear, he had fled from the threat of Jezebel, and, depressed and gloomy in mind through the prostration of his physical system, he felt that his mission had failed. The nation had utterly and entirely apostatized from God. The wicked blandishments of the masculine heathen queen and the consuming fires of persecution had burned the Church of God out of the land. Apparently, there were left "none but this Elijah, shining like a star in the great darkness." Therefore he preferred to die. But, in truth, there were seven thousand who had remained faithful to the true God.

I suspect the condition of the nation was then somewhat analogous to that of the English people in Reformation times. In England, different in this respect from Scotland and Geneva, and largely from Germany, the Reformation was predominantly a state and political movement; and a superficial reader of the history is astonished by the ease with which the nation seemed to change its opinions under Henry VIII., under Edward VI., under Mary, under Elizabeth, backward and forward from Romanism to a half-Protestantism, from semi-Protestantism to Romanism, and from Romanism to Protestantism again. But, says one of its historians, "We believe that the people whose minds were made up on either side, who were inclined to make any sacrifice or run any risk for either religion, were very few. Each side had a few enterprising champions and a few stout-hearted martyrs; but the nation, undetermined in its opinions and feelings, resigned itself implicitly to the guidance of the government, and lent to the sovereign for the time being an equally ready aid against either of the extreme parties. . . . In plain words, they did not think the difference between the hostile sects worth a struggle. There was undoubtedly a zealous Protestant party and a zealous Catholic party. But both these parties were, we believe, very small. We doubt whether both together made up at the time of Mary's death the twentieth part of the nation. The remaining nineteen-twentieths halted between the two opinions, and were not disposed to risk a revolution in the government for the purpose of giving to either of the extreme factions an advantage over the other."

Very much like this was the condition of

the Israelitish kingdom under Ahab. A small number, mainly foreigners from Sidon, under the fierce and imperious Jezebel, and those who depended upon her for preferment, were the fiery worshipers of Baal. The malign influence of the court was felt over the nation; and the masses swayed by it, neither decidedly the one thing nor the other, were halters between Jehovah and Baal. They went with the court, especially after the fires of persecution had raged against the followers of the true God. But still there was Obadiah, and there were the noble seven thousand, who made no show indeed publicly, who seem to have been the hidden ones of God, but who had not yielded to the false religion. And they were then the real Israel, the life-kernel in the hard shell of the nation. As it was then, so it has been and is. The ancient people were never fully cast away. Nor even yet are they in the flesh finally given up by God. They will be brought to the knowledge of Jesus, and be a great blessing to the Gentile churches.

"It is an unspeakable consolation to know that in times of deepest religious declension and most extensive defection from the truth the lamp of God has never been permitted to go out, and that a faithful remnant has ever existed—a remnant larger than their own drooping spirits could easily believe."

As Dean Stanley has emphasized it, this is a truth which, farther on and down in the kingdom of Judah, the greatest of all the prophets, who wrote for the Church in all ages, was commissioned to make specially prominent: "This is the true consolation of all ecclesiastical history. It is a thought which is but little recognized in its earlier and ruder stages, when the inward and outward are easily confounded together. But it is the very message of life to a more refined and complex age, and it was the keynote to the whole of Isaiah's prophecies. It had, indeed, been dimly indicated to Elijah in the promise of the few who had not bowed the knee to Baal, and in the still small whisper which was greater than thunder, earthquake and fire. But in Isaiah's time it first, if we may so say, became a living doctrine of the Jewish Church, and through him an inheritance of the Christian Church. '*A remnant*—the remnant.' (Isa. x. 20; xi. 11, 16; xxviii. 5.) This was his watchword. 'The remnant shall return. (*Shear-jashub*).' This was the truth constantly personified before him in the name of his eldest son. A remnant of good in the mass of corruption, a remnant saved from the destructive invasions of Assyria, a burst of spring-time in the reformation of Hezekiah; and, far away in the distant future, a Rod out of the stem, the wornout stem, of Jesse, a Branch, a faithful Branch, out of the withered root of David. 'And the wilderness and the solitary place shall be glad, and the desert shall rejoice and blossom as the rose; it shall blossom abundantly, even with joy and singing, and sorrow and sighing shall flee away.'"*

In the darkest days of the papal apostasy there were scattered through Europe many individuals and little organizations that bowed not the knee to the usurper of the Seven-hilled City—in Italy, among the Waldenses, through Germany, in Scotland and Ireland and England. They make little show in political records—no more than the seven thousand did in the history of Israel under Ahab.† They were not the ruling power. They were beaten down and despised. But they existed, and ever and anon their voice of protest was heard against the demoralizing corruption of popes and cardinals and priests and kings and people. "Where was your Church be-

---

* *History of the Jewish Church*, ii., 501, 502.

† One fact, however, that is made particularly prominent in the first volume of Green's new *Popular History of England*, is that the struggle against the papacy was in England unintermitted.

fore Luther's Reformation?" a Romanist once asked of a Protestant. "Where was your face before it was washed this morning?" was the shrewd reply. But, in fact, the retort did not express the full truth. There were reformers before the great Reformation. The time never was when true spiritual believers did not exist. Probably there was never a year when the Lord's Supper, as one of the great badges of the Church of Christ, was not observed in its pure and simple form and with its scriptural meaning.

Never are truth, virtue and religion without their advocates. Is there some error against which you feel you should wage war? some good work on which you feel you should enter? But do you fear you may be alone and your efforts will be fruitless? Be assured that if you will boldly resist the wrong and commence the work, you will have not only God on your side, but other associates. Even if alone, stand up for the right and the true, and you shall not remain alone. God has always kept a seed to serve him, and everywhere any one who continues faithful will find other congenial spirits.

And look! Amid the fearful apostasy of the court of Israel and the enervating influence of Jezebel over the public men of the nation—which was so strong that she could induce some of its elders to swear to a lie in order to murder Naboth, so that his vineyard might fall into Ahab's possession—there was, in the very house of the king, an Obadiah who feared the Lord and adhered to his worship. Whenever the conclusively exposed rascalities of men in office, and the more numerous false charges which like the frogs of Egypt creep over the land, tempt us to think that the whole generation of public men are corrupt, let us be reassured by Obadiah's case, and be hopeful that the noble and the honest have not died out.

(2.) The life and ministry of Elijah contain one striking illustration of the true catholicity which has always been a feature of the religion of the Bible.

When the drought and famine commenced in the Holy Land the prophet was directed by God to go to the heathen city of Sarepta, and to a poor widow who was living there, that he might be a blessing to her while partaking of her hospitality. He was sent away from his own land, from his own people, to one whom the Jews regarded as an outcast, that in her home he might spend the weary years of the national punishment.

To this fact Christ made a very pointed reference while he was upon the earth. The inhabitants of Nazareth, where he lived as a boy and a man before he began his public ministry, were among the last to credit him with anything supernatural. When they heard of his miracles in other places they were skeptical. "Is not this

Joseph's son?" they sneeringly asked after listening to some of his wonderfully gracious words in their own synagogue. His "long residence in Nazareth merely as a townsman had made him *too common*, incapacitating them for appreciating him as others did who were less familiar with his every-day demeanor in private life."* Therefore in a wrong spirit and in unbelief they wanted Capernaum's wonders done over again before them. But Jesus replied, "I tell you of a truth, many widows were in Israel in the days of Elias, when the heaven was shut up three years and six

---

* Brown's *Commentary*. How often does it happen that the nearest friends and the daily associates of a boy are the last to see anything extraordinary in him! One of the amusing touches in the biography of the historian Macaulay is found in an account of the way in which the nephews and nieces, with whom he romped in the home and acted like a big boy instead of a sedate man, had the idea to dawn upon their mind that their "Uncle Tom" was a great writer whose books the world was wild about. Even with the pure and divine Jesus the familiarity of the children and men and women of Nazareth bred contempt, and they could not imagine that he had miraculous power.

months, when great famine was throughout all the land; but unto none of them was Elias sent, save unto Sarepta, a city of Sidon, unto a woman that was a widow."

It would scarcely have been possible to utter a more stinging protest against the narrow uncharitableness which the Jews had engrafted upon their divinely-given religion. Looking upon themselves as peculiarly the chosen of God, and forgetting that they were chosen in trust for the salvation of the world, they were perpetually in danger of shutting out the Gentiles from saving mercy and of indulging the most merciless and uncharitable spirit toward them. But Jesus showed that the sovereign grace of God had not been restricted to the one nation. And, as a commentary in act upon that declaration, it is significant to note that he also went once into that heathen country of Sidon, and on the daughter of a countrywoman of the Sarepta widow performed one of his loving miracles; for the woman who came to him pleading for a daughter that had an unclean spirit, and who was willing, even as a dog, to have the crumbs that dropped from the children's hand, was a Syro-Phœnician.

Whether the widow of Sarepta had through contact with the Jewish truth become a worshiper of Jehovah before Elijah was sent to her, or whether she was then a heathen, and by daily contact with the prophet received that truth, she is an instance of a cheering principle which has its illustrations every here and there through the Old Testament. Too many Christians have been tempted to overlook it.

Never has salvation been confined to the visible Church. Least of all was it ever limited to the lineal descendants of Abraham. Job, perhaps contemporary with the father of the faithful, was a just and upright man before God and one of the redeemed elect, though not one of the ancient separated people.* Rahab of Jericho was brought from among the heathen into the

* "The moral of the book of Job is the noblest protest against, and the loftiest refutation of, those abuses or misapprehensions which might naturally flow from—which did flow from—the Mosaic and Jewish system. The relation of God to the Israelites as their special Sovereign, of the Israelites to God as his chosen and peculiar people, led almost of necessity to the vulgar notion (and the vulgar notion spread very widely) that Jehovah was the national God; a greater God, indeed, than the gods of the neighboring and hostile nations, but still self-limited, as it were, to be the tutelar deity of the sons of Abraham. Again, the temporal rewards and punishments of the Law were sure to lead —and did actually lead—to the conclusion that happiness and misery in this life were the one certain, undeniable test of the divine favor or disfavor. . . . What is the argument of the magnificent colloquies of Job and his comforters, of Elihu, and of the unrivalled close of the poem? The direct contradiction of these narrow conclusions—that God is the one universal God, that over the mysteries of his being, the mysteries of his providential government, there is the same impenetrable veil which shrouds the Godhead from the understanding of man. And all this, as seems most inevitable, is connected with the history—it may be the poetical and imaginative or the real history—of a man not a Jew; of a man (we cannot say whether he owes his fame to the poem or whether the poem was grounded on his fame) sprung from a race kindred to—and though at many periods in deadly hostility with—the Jews, yet owning a common ancestor—it may be, rather without doubt, speaking a kindred language."—*Milman's History of the Jews*, i., pp. 483, 484, *note.*

national organization and exalted to a peculiar place of honor in it as an ancestress of the Messiah. Ruth, the heathen Moabitess, was also providentially reached and placed upon the same honored roll.

Let us not hesitate consistently to apply the principle. Who can doubt that in the ancient world, outside the pale of the written revelation which was given to the nation from whose bosom the Messiah was to come in the fullness of time, traces of the prior revelation which God had written upon the human heart and given orally to the early fathers of the race remained widely spread; and that later still, by contact with the Jewish nation, the truths of its inspired books became the property of others; and that, through both these agencies, all over the heathen world men were led to live religious lives and to be accepted by God?*

* "Undoubtedly there was a valuable element of truth in the foundation of the system which was taught by the early Christian teachers of the Alexandrian school. They saw in the Greek philosophy not sheer error, but in one view a gift of God, and a

Let us believe that even now, while it is true that there is only the one name under heaven given among men whereby we must be saved, and that where the gospel is preached not a sinner who hears it can be saved without a penitent faith in him, yet as all who die in infancy are regenerated by the Spirit and saved through the efficacy of the atoning blood, so, wherever in the great mass of humanity God has any of his chosen, the same omnipotent Spirit reaches them for their salvation.

And let us, in our dealings with the irreligious, act under the influence of the spirit which sent Elijah to the Sarepta widow with the blessing of the unfailing meal and oil, and the Redeemer to the Syro-Phœnician sufferer with healing mercy. Restrict

theoretical schoolmaster for Christ, like the law in the practical sphere. . . . The elements of truth in the heathen philosophy they attributed partly to the secret operation of the Logos in the world of reason, partly to acquaintance with the Jewish philosophy, the writings of Moses and the prophets."—Schaff's *History of the Christian Church*, i., p. 497.

not benevolence and love to the Church. Within the ample folds of a true Christian charity embrace the unchristian, the antichristian, the irreligious, and the immoral, doing good to them as we have opportunity and seeking to bring them to the greatest and highest good of all.* So Jesus acted; and such should be the life of his disciples.

* This is not inconsistent with the sternest and strictest holding of the truth, and with a refusal to countenance errorists in their work. Dr. Culross, in his *John, whom Jesus Loved* (a charming book), commenting on the second epistle of John to the Elect Lady, says (pp. 169, 170): "The charge which John gives is an antidote to that so-called liberality to which truth and falsehood are alike, and which generally ends in hating truth with a murderous hatred. Whatever may be done from Christian compassion or kindness, let it be done without hesitation or fear, but let it be done as compassion or kindness—in the spirit of the good Samaritan. John finds no fault with it and throws no hindrance in its way. But keep the distinction clear between doing a deed of Christian beneficence and giving help to antichristian error. 'If there come any unto you, and bring not this doctrine, receive him not in your house, neither bid him God-speed; for he that biddeth him God-speed is partaker of his evil deeds.' There is a time for everything; and there is a time for crucifying mere good-nature as well as the lusts of the flesh."

(3.) More than upon any other life in the Old Testament the bright glow of immortality rests upon that of Elijah.

It has been contended that the Old Testament does not reveal immortality; that the future existence was not used in it as the crowning motive for the enforcement of a holy life; but that its inducements to morality are found in the influence of men's conduct on their present state of existence.

Now, it is very true that that earlier part of the divine revelation does specially lay hold of the principle that "godliness is profitable unto all things, having promise of the life that now is." It insists much upon the fact that true religion, including as that does true morality, has a legitimate tendency to keep the body in health, to give success in business, to lead to long life; and that vice saps the energy of soul and body, and is really death, slow and lingering—sometimes speedy—death. Along with the intensely devotional piety which glows in portions of it, and with the brilliant and far-reaching prophecies which peer down the ages, it is full of practical directions drawn from the present course of events. The charge which has been made against the philosophy of the ancient heathen world cannot be brought against the word of God. That philosophy "disdained to be useful and was content to be stationary. It dealt largely in theories of moral perfection which were so sublime that they could never be more than theories; in attempts to solve insoluble enigmas; in exhortations to the attainment of unattainable frames of mind. It could not condescend to the humble office of ministering to the comfort of human beings. All the schools contemned that office as degrading; some censured it as immoral. . . . What is the highest good, whether pain be an evil, whether all things be fated, whether we can be certain of anything, whether we can be certain that we are certain of nothing, whether a wise man can be unhappy, whether all departures from right be equally reprehensible,—these and other questions of the same sort occupied the brains, the tongues and the pens of the ablest men in the civilized world during several centuries."* The Bible, in both its great divisions, cut loose from such speculations. It revealed positive truth; it contained great facts. And it stated them in such a way as to fall in with the daily life of men from age to age, to give the foundation for true science and philosophy, and to anticipate the future progress of the human mind. The deepest and most advanced spiritual experience, under the full light of the gospel, finds in it language for its thorough expression; and even its references to other subjects are shown to be most wonderfully correct. A very recent scientific writer has stated that its "narrative of creation proves so accurate as to stand the test of facts discovered

---

* Macaulay's Essay on Lord Bacon.

long after it was written, and of scientific principles not established or thought of at that early time;" that "the order of creation as stated in Genesis is faultless in the light of modern science, and many of its details present the most remarkable agreement with the results of science born only in our own day;" and that this is in itself "a most powerful proof of its divine origin."* In truth, the book contains the principle of the inductive philosophy, with the enforcement and exaltation of which in modern times the name of Lord Bacon is indissolubly associated, and the application of which had given such a tremendous impulse to the world.

But while the present and the every-day practical do certainly stand out with special prominence in the moral system of the Old Testament; while the future is so much more clear and pervasive in the New Testament that it is declared Christ brought

* Dawson's *Nature and the Bible*, pp. 25, 26.

life and immortality to light through the gospel; while the firmament of the Old had not the brightness which the sun in his power now throws back over it from the New,—yet, as our Divine Master himself taught the Sadducees of his time, the truths of the immortal existence of the soul and of the resurrection of the body underlie the whole of revelation, and present the supreme and overruling motive for the purification of the life of earth.*

The public ministry of Elijah lies between two facts which most brilliantly bring this up to the surface and into the foreground. His chequered mission had in its beginning the enlivening light of a resurrection, and it closed in the brilliant glory of a translation.

Soon after he had been received as a guest in the lowly home of Sarepta the

* Indeed, without this there could have been no religion in the earlier period; for, as Max Müller says, "Without a belief in personal immortality religion is like an arch resting on one pillar, like a bridge ending in an abyss."

only son of his hostess died. Elijah cried to God, "O Lord, my God, I pray thee, let this child's soul come unto him again. And the Lord heard the voice of Elijah; and the soul of the child came unto him again, and he revived."

Look at the truths that are embodied in that touching narrative. A human being is composed of soul and body. It is the abiding of the soul in the body that gives life to the frame. What takes place at death is the departure of the soul from its tabernacle, not the cessation of the activity of the former nor the annihilation of the latter.

> "Cold in the dust this perished heart may lie,
> But that which warmed it once shall never die."

When it goes away it continues under the power of God. If he will bring it back, the body will revive.

This is the first resurrection recorded in the Bible. It rebukes the materialism, low and earthly, which denies that there is a soul essentially different from the body. And it points to the possibility of life being restored even after it has once been lost.

But where was the soul of that boy while the body was dead? Where are now the souls of the redeemed departed? The translation of the prophet has a bearing upon these questions, while it suggests the unending existence which even the bodies of the redeemed are to enjoy.

Centuries before, the pre-eminently pious Enoch had been translated that he should not see death. Suddenly, mysteriously, he disappeared from the midst of his fellows. He was not: for God took him.

To Elijah, God had made known his purpose in a like manner to honor and beatify him. In his despondency the prophet asked, under the juniper tree, that he might die—die there; die by the hand of the Almighty; die alone, a wretched failure, a disappointed man, scared, beaten, overcome by Jezebel. But God had better things in store for him. His prayers for drought and for rain had been answered. But that prayer for death was not granted. The refusal to answer a prayer is sometimes a greater evidence of divine love than would be the thing which is asked for. God's denials are answers.

To Elisha, also, and to the prophets at Bethel and at Jericho, God had made known this purpose. The favored man tested the devotion of his successor by urging him, as the time for the translation approached, to leave him alone. But Elisha would not be absent from such a glorious event. They therefore go on towards the river Jordan. The students in the prophetical schools stand and look from a distance. They see Elijah roll up his mantle into a staff and with it strike the waters and divide them, so that the two can walk together on dry ground. They see their great leader pass into the Jordan, as we now stand at the bedside of our beloved and see them go down into the flood. But Elisha is permitted to go farther and to see more. Faithful to the last, he is separated from Elijah only by a chariot of fire and horses of fire, while the latter, in soul and body, without seeing death, is borne aloft on a whirlwind "into heaven."

"Into heaven"! the place of the throne of God; the home of Jesus; the abode of the angels; the region of the universe which excels all others in brilliancy and splendor; the city of unspotted holiness and unmarred happiness. Thither Elijah was borne; thither went the Redeemer from the gaze of his apostles; thither goes every redeemed soul when at death it is taken out of the body; and from it at the last Jesus shall come with Enoch and Elijah and all glorified souls to wake from their long sleep the bodies that have been resting in their graves. "We are born for a higher destiny than that of earth; there is a realm where the rainbow never fades, where the stars will be spread before us like islands that slumber on the ocean, and where the beings that pass before us like shadows will stay in our presence for ever."

Under this life and immortality the whole Bible glows with an eternal brightness.

One night, eighteen hundred years ago, that magnificent brightness kissed the earth; for, when the Redeemer was transfigured on the mount, Elijah and Moses came from that place whence, in answer to Elijah's prayer, the soul of the widow's boy had come, and together, while the mount was illuminated by heaven's glory, they talked with him of the decease, or departure, or exodus which he was to accomplish at Jerusalem.

The redeeming Son of God had come forth from the Father and had come into the world; again, he was to leave the world and go to the Father. He, too, soul and body transformed and glorified, as the type and leader of his people, was to be carried up on the clouds to the throne of heaven. But first he was to go to death—to the ignominious death of the cross, and down from that to the rough waters of the Jordan. Just as surely, however, as he should die and rise again and ascend to ecstatic bliss, so should all who put their trust in him and follow him be kept in death, be brought forth from death, and be blessed with the translation of Enoch and Elijah and Jesus himself.

Sinful soul! Exposed at any and every moment to the visit of the death-angel, make your future sure and glorious by receiving your salvation through the sacrifice of the Crucified One, and by commencing that Christian life which at last is glorified in the unutterable brilliancy of heaven. The sooner in life this is done the better, and the less of even selfish sacrifice is called for. There is an old Persian fable which may illustrate one sad effect of a sinful course: "King Zohak gave the devil leave to kiss his shoulders. Instantly two serpents sprang out, who, in the fury of anger, attacked his head and attempted to get at his brain. Zohak pulled them away and tore them with his nails. But he found that they were inseparable parts of himself, and that what he was lacerating was his own flesh"! Give Satan leave to kiss you; yield to his seductive temptations; and vices will burst out from your system and devour your very life; yea, they will so become a part of your being itself after long indulgence that the effort, when made, to break loose from them and to tear them out and cast them away, will be sharp and harrowing: it will be tearing away what has become a part of the sinful self. Better never to come under their power! Better not to yield to Satan's overtures. If they have been indulged at all, better, without longer indulgence, to break loose from the evil, and day by day to be found in that manner of life which necessitates no convulsive, painful revolution, but which is always ready for the summons from above.

Remember, Christian believer, that the true way to be ready for death is to be found at your appointed work, whatever it may be, in its own time. How expressive the record about Elijah and Elisha! "It came to pass as they still walked on *and talked*, that behold there appeared a chariot of fire and horses of fire and parted them both asunder; and Elijah went up by a whirlwind into heaven." As Bishop Hall remarks, "Surely that conference was needful, and upon matters of high importance to the Church and the nation, in connection with the promises of their covenant God; otherwise we might have expected it would have given way to private meditation, and

Elijah had been taken up rather from his knees than from his feet. But there can be no better posture or state for the messenger of our dissolution to find us in than in a diligent prosecution of our calling. The busy attendance on our holy vocation is no less pleasing to God than an immediate devotion.

"Devotion is a part of the religious life. Reading the Bible, meditation, prayer, communion with God in the closet, in the family, in the church, are necessary and valuable religious duties. But they are not the whole of religion. That extends out through the daily conduct and into every relation of life. Faithful therein the servant of God should be; and if the death-messenger finds him faithful in it, blessed is he! For then the ravishing splendor, the enrapturing magnificence, the ecstatic joy, into which the soul passes! 'Now we see through a glass darkly; but then face to face.'"

In the chariot and horses of fire that came down to Elijah; in the brightness that encompassed him as he ascended; in the entrancing descriptions of revelation which give us some glimpses through the open door of heaven; we see enough to thrill our hearts and make us long for the full enjoyment of it. But how little of it we really grasp! How faint our conception of it, with all our study and all our meditation, compared to that which, in a moment, in the twinkling of an eye, bursts upon the souls of those who fall asleep in Jesus, and by the angels are, as with an electric flash, borne into his glorious presence!

"Charming thought, my brethren, of the change that death shall produce in us," cries out an old French preacher; "it shall supersede the puerilities of infancy; it shall draw the curtain which conceals the objects of expectation. How ravished must the soul be when this curtain is uplifted! Instead of worshiping in these assemblies, it finds itself instantly elevated to the choirs of angels, the ten thousand times ten thousand before the Lord. Instead of hearing the hymns we sing to his glory, it instantly hears the hallelujahs of celestial spirits and the dread shouts of 'Holy, holy, holy is the Lord of hosts, the whole earth is full of his glory!' Instead of listening to this frail preacher, who endeavors to develop the imperfect notions he has imbibed in a confined understanding, it instantly hears the great Head of the Church, who is the Author and Finisher of our faith. Instead of perceiving some traces of God's perfections in the beauties of nature, it finds itself in the midst of his sublimest works, in the midst of the heavenly Jerusalem whose gates are of pearl, whose foundations are of precious stones, and whose walls are of jasper. Do we then, still fear death? And have we still need of comforters when we approach that happy period? And have we still need to resume all our constancy and all our fortitude to support the idea of dying? And is it still necessary to pluck us from the earth, and to tear us by force to the celestial abode which shall consummate our felicity? Ah, how the prophet Elisha, who saw his Master ascend in the chariot of fire, ploughing the air on his brilliant throne, and crossing the vast expanse which separates heaven from earth,—how Elisha regretted the absence of so worthy a master, whom he now saw no more, and whom he must never see in life! how he cried in that moment, 'My father, my father, the chariot of Israel and the horsemen thereof!'

"These emotions are strikingly congenial to the sentiments of self-love so dear to us. But Elijah himself—did he fear to soar in so sublime a course? Elijah, already ascended to the middle regions of the air, in whose eyes the earth appeared but as an atom retiring out of sight; Elijah, whose head already reached to heaven,—did Elijah regret the transition he was about to complete? Did he regret the world and its inhabitants? O soul of man, regenerate soul! daily called to break the fetters which unite thee to a mortal body, take thy flight toward heaven. Ascend this fiery chariot which God has sent to transport thee above the earth where thou dwellest. See the heavens which open for thy reception; admire the beauties and estimate the charms already realized by thy hope. Taste those ineffable delights. Anticipate the perfect felicity with which death is about to invest thee. Death himself is about to do all the rest—to dissipate all thy darkness and to crown thy hopes."*

* Saurin's *Sermons*, i., p. 362.

V.
CHARACTER AND TRAINING OF THE MAN.

THE last words of the Old Testament, resplendent with the glory of the predicted Messiah, make this promise: "Behold, I will send you Elijah the prophet before the coming of the great and dreadful day of the Lord. And he shall turn the heart of the fathers to the children, and the heart of the children to their fathers, lest I come and smite the earth with a curse." Mal. iv. 5, 6.

This led to the expectation of a bodily return by the great prophet of fire to the earth before the Christ should come. Under it the Jewish mind also dwelt in a peculiar manner upon Elijah. "It was a fixed belief of the Jews that he had appeared again and again, as an Arabian merchant, to wise and good rabbis at their prayers or on their journeys. A seat is placed for him to superintend the circumcision of the Jewish children. Passover after passover the Jews of our own day place the paschal cup on the table and set the door wide open, believing that that is the moment when Elijah will reappear. When goods are found and no owner comes, when difficulties arise and no solution appears, the answer is, 'Put them away until Elijah comes.' " *

* Stanley's *Jewish Church*, ii., pp. 321, 322. Milman's remark (in *Hist. of the Jews*, i., p. 401) is worth emphasizing: " The memory of Elijah as the great type and representative of the prophetic order sank deep into the hearts of the Jewish people. It was remarkable that a prophet who lived entirely in the revolted kingdom, among the ancestors of the Samaritans—who, as far as we know, never set his foot in Jerusalem—who is never known to have written a word—to whom were ascribed none of their wonderful prophetic poems—should be received by later Jewish tradition as the prophet, as the forerunner and harbinger of the Messiah." Under the divine guidance which led to this, it is an illustration, of the better kind, of a remark of Macaulay

On two separate occasions our Divine Redeemer explained the meaning of the
in his *Essays*, v., p. 500 : " Some individual is selected, and often selected very injudiciously, as the representative of every great movement of the public mind, of every great revolution in human affairs ; and on this individual are concentrated all the love and all the hatred, all the admiration and all the contempt, which he ought rightfully to share with a whole party, a whole sect, a whole nation, a whole generation." The French Renan, with his accustomed naturalistic lowering, says : ". Since the Jewish nation, in a kind of despair, had taken to reflecting upon its destiny, the imagination of the people had directed itself with affectionate concentration to the ancient prophets. Now, of all the personages of the past whose memory came like a dream in the night to agitate and excite the nation, the greatest was Elijah. This giant among the prophets in his savage solitude on Carmel, sharing the life of wild beasts, dwelling in the hollows of the rocks, whence from time to time he descended like a thunderbolt to make and unmake kings, had become, by a series of successive metamorphoses, a kind of supernatural being, sometimes visible, sometimes invisible, who had never tasted death. It was a general belief that Elijah would return and restore Israel. The austere life he had led, the terrible memories which he had left, and which still abide in the imagination of the East (Abdallah, the ferocious pasha of Acre, nearly died of fright after beholding the prophet in a dream standing on the mount; in the pictures of the Christian churches the portrait of Elijah is surrounded with severed heads, and the Mussulmans themselves fear him); his threatening image, which even now seems to spread terror and death, his whole legend, full of vengeance and fear, produced a

prediction and the sense in which the prophet was to reappear.

John the Baptist, after he had been cast into prison by Herod, sent two of his disciples to Jesus with an impatient, almost a despairing, message, which was evidently designed to call forth an explicit assertion of his Messiahship, and perhaps an interposition of the divine power for his own deliverance from prison. "Art thou he that should come? or look we for another?" "It seemed no doubt hard to him that his Master should let him lie so long in prison for his fidelity — useless to his Master's cause and a comparative stranger to his proceedings — after having been honored to

lively impression on the mind, and stamped, as it were, a birth-mark on the results of popular throes. Whosoever aspired to active eminence among the people was bound to imitate Elijah; and, as the solitary life had been the distinguishing peculiarity of this prophet, it became customary to look on 'the man of God' as a hermit. It was imagined that all holy personages had had their period of penance, of austerity, of life in regions far from towns; and a retirement to the desert became thus the condition and prelude of lofty destinies."

announce and introduce him to his work and to the people. And since the wonders of his hand seemed only to increase in glory as he advanced, and it could not but be easy for him who preached deliverance to the captives and the opening of the prison to them that were bound, to put it into the heart of Herod to set him at liberty or to effect his liberation in spite of him, he at length determines to see if, through a message from the prison by his disciples, he cannot get Jesus to speak out his mind, and at least set his own at rest. . . . The message itself, indeed, was far from a proper one. It was peevish; it was presumptuous; it was all but desperate. He had become depressed; he was losing heart; his spirit was clouded; heaven's sweet light had to some extent departed from him; and this message was the consequence." * Having sent the messengers back with his answer, Jesus pro-

* Brown on Luke.

nounced a noble eulogy on John, closing it with the assertion, "If ye will receive it, this is Elias which was for to come." Matt. xi. 14.

Again, after the transfiguration of our Redeemer, in response to a reference to his coming death, the three disciples who had been with him on the mount asked, "Why, then, say the scribes that Elias must first come? And Jesus answered and said unto them, Elias truly shall first come and restore all things. But I say unto you that Elias is come already, and they knew him not, but have done unto him whatsoever they listed. Likewise shall also the Son of man suffer of them. Then the disciples understood that he spake unto them of John the Baptist."

Elijah thus reappeared in John—not personally, not bodily, but because, as the angel declared in advance to Zachariah the father of the Forerunner, he should go before Jesus "in the spirit and power of

Elias." He was to be the same kind of a man; he was to do the same kind of a work; he was to be, in character and in the kingdom of heaven, the successor of the old prophet of Ahab's days.

No more splendid encomium could be pronounced upon either than to say that he was the peer of the other.

In this volume I have given a pictorial panorama of the life of Elijah, and have exhibited three series of the grand lessons for our own days which are suggested by the great events of his ministry. I will now attempt to analyze and portray the character of the man who was so singularly favored by God—the spirit and the power of one who shines so brightly in the kingdom of heaven; the features of his person, physical, mental and spiritual, which we should take as a model.

"There is something supremely bracing in coming in contact with a noble and chivalrous life. When for a moment we leave the meanness, earthliness and selfishness which in so great a measure make up the every-day world, and rise, though in imagination only, into sympathy with the high aims and unshaken will of some heroic saint of God, we receive an impression of the value of righteousness and trust which no mere human statement can convey. It is like going from the noise and drudgery of the streets to the majesty and free air of the mountains. We may not be able to express in words what we feel, and why we feel, but feel we do, the power, grandeur, glory of the infinite. And thus it is that the Bible contains more of biography than of abstract doctrine; for the highest and most absolute truths not only become simple and pass current in the world when clothed in the flesh and blood of human history, but they attain power by awakening sympathy. As the grasp of a hand or the flash of an eye is often the most eloquent interpreter of goodness, so a life truly lived will impress the world better and more lastingly than all the dry axioms of duty ever penned."

In the atmosphere of such lives we ought to try to live. By their example we should be stimulated and guided, seeking to avoid their sins and weaknesses and to reproduce their strength and virtues. The fault of many is that they do not endeavor to copy any such high standards. "A man who has never seen the sun," says an old writer, "cannot be blamed for thinking that no glory can exceed that of the moon. The man who has seen neither moon nor sun cannot be blamed for talking of the unrivalled brightness of the morning star." One who has not had the opportunity to become acquainted with the higher lives of earth may be excused for stopping at lower models; but if the higher are within view and imitation, contentment with a lower is inexcusable. "Be ye followers of me," says Paul, "even as I also of Christ."

If any should be tempted to think that because Elijah was a prophet and inspired he was placed on a plane too high for imitation, let it be remembered that he is emphatically declared to have been a man "subject to like passions as we are."

It has been very aptly said that "there is in one respect a remarkable analogy between the faces and the minds of men. No two faces are alike; and yet very few faces deviate very widely from the common standard." Among the hundreds of thousands of human beings who inhabit a large city there is not one who will be taken on close inspection by his acquaintances for another; yet a man may walk from one limit of it to the other without seeing one person in whom any feature is so overcharged that he will turn to stare at it. Such cases there are, but they are rarely met with. "An infinite number of varieties lies between limits which are not very far asunder. The specimens which pass those limits on either side form a very small minority. It is the same with the characters of men. Here, too, the varieties pass all enumeration. But the cases in which the deviation from the common standard is striking and grotesque are very few. In one mind avarice predominates; in another, pride; in a third, love of pleasure: just as in one countenance the nose is the most marked feature, while in others the chief expression lies in the brow or in the lines of the mouth. But there are very few countenances in which nose, brow and mouth do not contribute, though in an unequal degree, to the general effect; and so there are very few characters in which one overgrown propensity makes all others utterly insignificant." Perhaps the common notion is that "every man has one ruling passion, and that this clue, once known, unravels all the mysteries of his conduct." But, in general, human beings are "made up of a crowd of passions, which contend for the mastery over them and govern them in turn." They live "not under the absolute dominion of one despotic propensity, but under a mixed government in which a hundred powers balance each other." *

In the character of Elijah, as it is reflected from the sacred pages, there was one overruling and absorbing passion which marked him as the great representative of the prophets of Israel. That was an exclusive and overmastering devotion to God. It will be inspiring to see how this supreme devotion manifested itself, and how it was sustained.

(1.) He was pre-eminently a righteous man. This is suggested in a significant manner by the reference which the apostle James makes to him; for after having said, "The effectual fervent prayer of a righteous man availeth much," he immediately adds: "Elias was a man subject to like

* Macaulay's *Essays*, v., pp. 304, 307.

passions as we are, and he prayed earnestly that it might not rain: and it rained not on the earth by the space of three years and six months. And he prayed again, and the heaven gave rain and the earth brought forth her fruit." Two such answers to prayer indicated that Elijah was one of those peculiarly righteous men whose energetic petitions have remarkable power in the court of heaven. The workings of nature are under the constant control and guidance of God. He is the great Force of the universe, underlying, energizing, and directing the motion of matter and of spirit, which in its conservation and correlation produces the changes that are perpetually in progress on the field of creation. Between the human mind and the almighty Ruler of the universe there are a communion and a mutual influence which can affect the daily working of the elements and of nature in all her departments. The firmament is "not a vault of brass interposed between us and the higher heavens." Men of peculiar sanctity and energy of spirit have access to the divine throne. They have power with God; having power with God, they exert an influence over the world of matter and of spirit; and in emergencies when God designs to use the natural forces as the handmaids of his providence and grace, his Spirit prompts such souls to their energetic wrestling with him; and so the almighty Force works down, and draws up, and flashes forth, in transmutations of energy which accomplish the divine purpose, without jarring or disturbing the balance of power in the material and spiritual world.

The righteous man is right toward God through a penitent faith in his saving promises and sincere obedience to his commands; and he is right in his dealings with his fellows.

The record of Elijah's life which has been handed down to us contains only a few of the incidents of his ministry. If we knew more about him, we should doubtless find that in his private conduct and in his several social relations he was a man of great purity and correctness. Whatsoever things were true, whatsoever things were honest, whatsoever things were just, whatsoever things were pure, whatsoever things were lovely, whatsoever things were of good report, were found in him.

But the element of his righteousness which is made prominent in the history is that which he had toward God, and which when real always includes the human aspect of it as a necessity. His simple faith in Jehovah and prompt obedience to him never wavered. When despondent through a mistaken conviction of the failure of his mission, he never thought of yielding to Jezebel and becoming a worshiper of Baal. With all the adverse influences that surrounded him, and even when he thought he stood alone, his faith faltered not. He was not a reed shaken with the wind. He was not clothed in soft raiment, gorgeously appareled and living delicately in the king's court as a sycophantic adherent of the false religion that would have brought him political honor and worldly riches. "Alone!" Well, he could stand alone. It could not be said of him that "he resembled those creepers which must lean on something and which, as soon as their prop is removed, fall down in utter helplessness;" and that "he could no more stand up erect and self-supported in any cause than the ivy can rear itself like the oak or the wild vine shoot to heaven like the cedar of Lebanon." He was not a creeper, not an ivy, not a vine; but an oak, a cedar, standing majestically erect in the abandoned and burnt-up kingdom of Ahab. A noble man, indeed, for imitation in this age.

There are men in whom "the impulse which drives them from a party in adversity to a party in prosperity is as irresistible as that which drives the cuckoo and the swallow toward the sun when the dark and cold months are approaching." Elijah was none of these. From the beginning to the end, against all temptations, all blandishments, all threats, all dangers, and under all apparent discouragements, he adhered to his God and to his religion. His opinions "did not spin round like a weathercock in a whirlwind." He stood firmly by his faith, with his eye toward God; and because he stood thus alone he stood the more firmly; for it is the nature of true piety to be strengthened and toughened by the temptations which do not uproot and destroy it. The storms that assail, root it more tenaciously in the soil.

(2.) The righteousness and holiness which were developed in Elijah were peculiarly active in their manifestations.

There is a passive piety which is very lovely, and sometimes has a delightful influence for the cause of God. Frequently it has a constitutional basis. On souls meek, quiet, comparatively listless by nature, grace is engrafted in a gentle way which does not revolutionize the individual peculiarities, but simply directs them in the line of thoughtful and gentle meditation on spiritual things. Occasionally, natures that have been stormy, impulsive, fiery, are subdued into it by heavy afflictions which the Spirit of God has used with a saving effect.

But this passive piety, sweet, gentle, attractive as it is in the home and social circle, happy as it is for some souls, having a place as it doubtless has in the kingdom of God, is not the kind which fights the heaviest battles for God, and gives the grandest impulse to his work, and stems the progress of vice and irreligion. The more active type is needed.

And it was the active, combative, fervent, military piety that Elijah possessed. He was jealous for the Lord, whose authority had been set at naught in the kingdom. He exhibited a burning and fierce zeal against idolatry and wrong. His whole appearance, stern and rugged, suggested this; and the great crises of his life were those in which he came forth to manifest it as with the very power of God. He could not be content with quietly enjoying the true religion himself while those around him were departing from it and sinning against their God. Time and again, in the strength of his faith and the fervor of his zeal, he came forward to endeavor to stem the current and to turn the transgressors to the Lord. With the purity of his private life he united the high purpose and the burning zeal of the reformer; and of course none but a man of private purity has the right to be a public reformer.

But this high and overmastering jealousy for God, and this stern resistance to error, were not dissociated from a gentle disposition in Elijah. The gentler element of the heart flows as an under-current through his life, and on more than one occasion ripples above the surface. The larger part of his ministry, in the providence of God, seemed to be of the severe cast; but at the very beginning of it, in the home at Sarepta, an incident happened which revealed "at once the tenderness of the prophet and how great the burden was to him of being apparently the instrument of judgment wherever he went. The widow's son dies, and he is reproached for it by the unhappy mother. Must he then be the harbinger of nothing but sorrow? In bitterness of soul he lifts the dead body from the bosom of the mother, carries it up to the upper room where he abode, lays it on his own bed, and in a perfect agony of prayer beseeches God to have mercy on him and let the child live. So deeply is his being stirred that three times over he stretches himself on the corpse with strong crying; and the Lord heard him."

The union of jealous zeal for God and of sternness in the public maintenance of the truth, with tenderness and gentleness of heart in the home, and even toward transgressors whom it is a duty to resist, is not rare. Nay, it is one of the marks of a truly well-balanced mind.

In the days of the English Restoration, when prelacy and immorality on the throne united in the persecution of dissenters, John Bunyan was imprisoned for preaching. "He was told that if he would give up preaching he should be instantly liberated. He was warned that if he persisted in disobeying the law he would be liable to banishment, and that if he were found in England after a certain time his neck would be stretched. His answer was, 'If you let me out to-day I will preach again to-morrow.' Year after year he lay patiently in a dungeon compared with which the worst prison now to be found in the island is a palace. His fortitude is the more extraordinary because his domestic feelings were unusually strong. Indeed, he was considered by his stern brethren as somewhat too fond and indulgent a parent. He had several small children, and among them a daughter who was blind, and whom he loved with peculiar tenderness. He could not, he said, bear even the wind to blow on her; and now she must suffer cold and hunger; she must beg; she must be beaten. 'Yet,' he added, 'I must, I must do it.'" The weakness of our day is that we have not too much of the tenderness, but too little of the overmastering zeal.

(3.) The intrepid courage which Elijah exhibited is the crowning element of his character. His unwavering faith and his burning zeal, under the direction of the Most High, brought him in collision with the reigning sentiment of his day; but with a dauntless boldness he resisted and denounced wrong.

There are men whose temporary safety and advancement in stirring times are found in their "levity and apathy." They are like "those light Indian boats which are safe because they are pliant, which yield to the impact of every wave, and which therefore bound without danger through a surf in which a vessel ribbed with heart of oak would inevitably perish." Generally, men who have no strongly-settled moral principles, but who are genial and deferential to everybody, who fall in with the humors of the day and the views of those that they have to deal with, are, even though vicious and dishonest, very popular with the greater number. It is strange, but true, that the easy-living and generous man, even though his generosity may be at the expense of others, is more apt to be liked than the sternly just, honest, truthful man, who may not be as serpentine in his manners, as easy in his disposition, as free in his bounty. The profligate Aaron Burr was in his day wonderfully popular with fashionable ladies and with the brainless multitude, because his courtesy was very winning and his disposition liberal and generous, especially in vice and toward the vicious.

Elijah was none of these easy men. He yielded not a hair's breadth to error; nor did he float with the current of sin. Moreover, he did not belong to "that section of society which in its dealings with gilded arrogance takes very good care not to err on the side of intolerance." He was very intolerant of sin and of the false religion which cursed his land. The magnificence of his courage was exhibited in the fact that his sternest denunciations were not against the poor, the low, the powerless, who could not, if they would, injure him. That is a poor kind of faithfulness to the truth, and a contemptible weakness, which can denounce sin in the abstract, but deal tenderly with particular forms of sin; which can score transgressions that are committed in other congregations or neighborhoods or times, but let the iniquities prevalent among those who are listening to the speaker go scot free; which can buffet children and women and uninfluential persons who cannot resist or answer, but pass over the heads of mighty men that may be in a position to annoy the speaker. That was not Elijah's style of courage. He dared to resist the king and to tell him that *he* was the troubler of Israel, and to sentence him and his house to infamous deaths for his crime against Naboth. He dared to expostulate with the representatives of the nation because they were disgraceful halters between the true and the false. He dared to go to the palace of Ahaziah and tell him that for his sin he should never come down from his bed of sickness.

This faithful courage is what the world ever needs. Nathan had it when, addressing the transgressing David, after evoking from his own conscience a condemnation of the act into which he had fallen, he said with pointed finger, "Thou art the man." John the Baptist had it when he told King Herod that it was not lawful for him to be living with his brother's wife; and thereby brought upon himself the deadly anger of the abandoned woman. Peter and John had it when they told the Jewish Sanhedrim that it was their duty to obey God rather than man. Luther had it when he said that he would go to Worms and declare the truth to the emperor and princes that were assembled there, though he should meet with as many devils as there were tiles on the house-tops. John Knox had it when he resisted the beautiful but false queen, and saved Scotland from the seven-hilled tyranny; and discharged his ministry in such a way that when he died the regent Morton pronounced over his coffin the eulogy, "Here lies one who never feared the face of man!" Glorious John Knox! stronger than Elijah in this: the idolatrous Jezebel did once frighten Elijah; John never quailed before the Romish Mary.

The minister of the gospel who would speak sharply to the poor, but with velvet tongue to the rich transgressors, who would not tell the same truth to a congressman, or president, or king, that he would to the beggar, degrades his calling. And the private Christian who will not meekly, tenderly, lovingly though decidedly, resist wrong wherever it breaks forth, fails in the highest development of the Christian character.

The man who has such courage as this will not be popular while he lives. Reformers and plain-spoken denouncers of wrong seldom are popular while upon the scene of action. From a distance and after their death they are exceedingly admired, but they grate terribly on those whose errors they have to combat. Ahab and Jezebel did not like Elijah.

The noble character which was thus exhibited by Elijah was of course the work of the Spirit of God. But there were two sources of power which were very influentially used in the development of it.

(1.) It is evident that the prophet was a man of great physical strength and endurance. With a healthy and muscular frame, he was able on the evening of the day on which the struggle upon Mount Carmel was waged, and after all the weary excitement of that day, to run beside the chariot of Ahab from Carmel to Jezreel, a distance of at least fourteen miles, keeping up with the horses all the way. The man who could do that must have had a sinewy and tough body.

Now, the physical frame has a great influence on the development of the mind and on spiritual exercises. There have been cases in which very weak and blasted frames have contained powerful and sharp minds, though in such cases there has been a warp in the mind which has given it and its associates much unhappiness.

For a time one of the most influential—but to those who have read his private life one of the most contemptible—of the adversaries of Christianity was the French Voltaire. "The constitution of his mind resembled the constitution of those bodies in which the slightest scratch of a bramble or the bite of a gnat never fails to fester. . . . Though he enjoyed during his own lifetime the reputation of a classic; though he was extolled by his contemporaries above all poets, philosophers and historians; though his works were read with as much delight and admiration at Moscow and Westminster, at Florence and Stockholm, as at Paris itself, he was tormented by that restless jealousy which should seem to belong only to minds burning with the desire of fame and yet conscious of impotence."*

At the other extreme, Dr. Samuel Johnson had "an unsound mind and an unsound body; great muscular strength, accompanied by much awkwardness and many infirmities; great weakness of parts, and a morbid propensity to slowness and procrastination; a kind and generous heart and a gloomy and irritable temper. . . . His whole life was darkened by the shadow of death; and he never thought of the inevitable future without horror." Yet "when at length the moment, dreaded through so many years, came close, the dark cloud passed away from his mind. His temper became unusually patient and gentle; he ceased to think with terror of death; and he spoke much of the mercy of God and the propitiation of Christ. . . . The light

* Macaulay's *Essays*, v., p. 194.

from heaven shone on him indeed, but not in a direct line or with its own pure splendor. The rays had to struggle through a disturbing medium; they reached him refracted, dulled, and discolored by the thick gloom which had settled on his soul; and though they might be sufficiently clear to guide him, they were too dim to cheer him." *

But, generally, a tainted, weak, suffering body enervates the mind; a healthy body gives tone to mental exercises; though there are exceptions enough to the remark to destroy the materialistic idea that the physical and mental forces are correlated. A regenerate soul will have its freedom of action and its healthy development, under the influence of the Holy Spirit, wonderfully assisted by a strong physical system. Something of Elijah's equable faith, unflagging zeal, and high courage was due to the splendid frame which he brought from his

* Macaulay's *Essays*, vi., p. 172.

youthful life beyond the Jordan, and kept and strengthened by his temperate mode of living. He was not one of your filigree men, "pretty to look at, but too brittle to bear the slightest pressure."

Nerves are one of the penalties which we pay for an advancing civilization. Savages are not annoyed by them. Hardworking people among ourselves do not suffer much from them. They afflict especially three classes: persons in whom the weakness is hereditary; those who have not steady and hard work in company with others, but have time for listless novel-reading and unhealthful introspection; and literary men, who are proverbially sensitive. Persons of all these classes, whose habits are sedentary, and whose business it is to attend to sufferers and to become the recipients of their woes, are more in danger of morbid mental exercises than others. They know what a blessing it would be to have a strong, tough body.

Of course, an entirely different class—and very blamable—are those who by the practice of vices voluntarily weaken the body, and thus, too, harm the mind.

"To keep the body in temperance, soberness and chastity, to guard it from pernicious influences, and to obey the laws of health, are just as much religious as they are moral duties."

Especially would I emphasize the duty, for the preservation of a sound body, of abstinence from intoxicating liquors. As John the Baptist never touched them, so Elijah, his great type, never did. They poison the physical system; they undermine and weaken it; therefore it is wrong to drink them or to have anything to do with them. Death is in the cup. If you want to keep bright and healthy and sound, let it alone.

(2.) While Elijah preserved his physical strength, he developed his soul as well by frequent seasons of private meditation and communion with God in prayer. He had the passive piety which consists in that meditative and prayerful communion with the Most High; and in that was rooted his strong active piety. The two are essential each to the healthy development of the other. The Christian in whom the two are beautifully and efficiently blended is the nearest to perfection.

This habit of communion with the Divine throws a bright glow over Elijah's whole ministry. His first appearance is as a man who had been energetically praying to God, and had been commissioned to declare to Israel's king that the prayer was about to be answered by a terrible judgment upon the land. In the little room of the widow of Sarepta he is again revealed as a wrestler with God in prayer. At the close of the Mount Carmel contest he occupies the attitude of supplication to God, while he directs his servant to go and go again seven times to look for the coming rain. He did not live constantly in the eye of the public. He frequently withdrew from the gaze of others, and by himself, or in company with his select associates, was making spiritual improvement.

Frequent rest from labor is a necessity for any and every person—a necessity for bodily health and mental strength. Hence the incalculable value of the Sabbath as a simple sanitary measure. As one of the most brilliant of Englishmen—who does not, however, appear to have had a sufficiently exalted spiritual view of the day—once declared in Parliament: "The natural difference between Campania and Spitzbergen is trifling when compared with the difference between a country inhabited by men full of bodily and mental vigor and a country inhabited by men sunk in bodily and mental decrepitude. Therefore it is that we are not poorer, but richer, because we have through many ages rested from our labor one day in seven. That day is not lost. While industry is suspended; while the plough lies in the furrow; while the exchange is silent; while no smoke ascends from the factory,—a process is going on quite as important to the wealth of nations as any process which is performed on more busy days. Man, the machine of machines, the machine compared with which all the contrivances of the Watts and the Arkwrights are worthless, is repairing and winding up, so that he returns to his labors on the Monday with clearer intellect, with livelier spirits, with renewed corporal vigor." *

Unite with the weekly physical rest the improvement of the soul by the study of God's word, and by loving, prayerful communion with him in private; add to it briefer seasons of such intercourse with the Most High before commencing and on closing the secular duties of each day; and

* *Life and Letters of Macaulay*, ii., p. 157.

you keep pouring on the divine oil which both lubricates the mental and physical machine and nourishes the fire of faith, zeal and courage for God. Thus was the peerless soul of Elijah made a worthy occupant of his matchless body.

So the grand old prophet appears before us: a man who, with a strong physical frame, had, by prayerful communion with God, under divine grace, developed his spiritual character into a steady, serene faith which held fast to God and his worship amid the abounding apostasy of his day, and a consistent piety in his intercourse with his fellows; into a burning zeal for the truth which made him set his face like a flint against irreligion and immorality; and into an intrepid courage which enabled him to rebuke the high and the mighty, and in the end to recover his nation from the odious idolatry into which it had fallen.

Such as he was, but toned by the full and the gentler influences of the gospel, in the essentials of his mission, and without its wrathful flashings, should all ministers be; and as all ministers, so all Christians in their various spheres.

You may not be blessed with the strong, the tough, the healthy, physical frame which Elijah had. It may be your lot to have had transmitted to you an organization weakened from the beginning in its very germ. Or, beneath what you have passed through —perhaps innocent, perhaps guilty on your part—your body may have been shattered and broken into a peculiar nervousness and sensitiveness, which at times clouds some of your spiritual exercises, or destroys the healthy and regular vigor of the mind. And, with that, you cannot endure as much as Elijah could, nor have the steady and serene peace which, with one exception, appears to have characterized his life.

But you should guard against practices

which weaken the body still more; or if blessed with a sound frame, you should guard against the habits and indulgences which have a tendency to ruin it. You should, by frequent meditation on the truth of God and prayerful communion with him, increase the spiritual life of the soul. You should, by friendly communion with other true Christians and with Christ himself, quicken its manifestations. You should have a sincere and honest faith in God, a steady and burning zeal for him, and an unwavering courage to stand up for his truth, and to resist whatever wrong may cross your path.

These things all should have. Ay, and in a higher degree than Elijah had; for as Christ said of John, who had his spirit and power, the least in the kingdom of heaven is greater than he. With the full gospel light we are more favorably situated than he was, and should show even a nobler religious life.

Settle not down into a selfish inactivity, if you are not in a high position and have not some great mission to fulfill. Because you think you cannot do heroic things, neglect not the little that you can do. Wherever God has placed you—and as you rise higher in life—if his providence so exalts you, in heart and in conduct; in your home and social circle; in overcoming your own sins and battling against the seductions of the world and the temptations of Satan; in tenderness toward the suffering and in stern resistance to oppressors and wrong-doers; in sympathy with your fellows and in single-hearted devotion to your God and Redeemer,—seek to exhibit

The Spirit and Power of Elias.

THE END.

www.ingramcontent.com/pod-product-compliance
Lightning Source LLC
Chambersburg PA
CBHW020815230426
43666CB00007B/1026